Tales of Krishna

The Divine Cowherd Boy

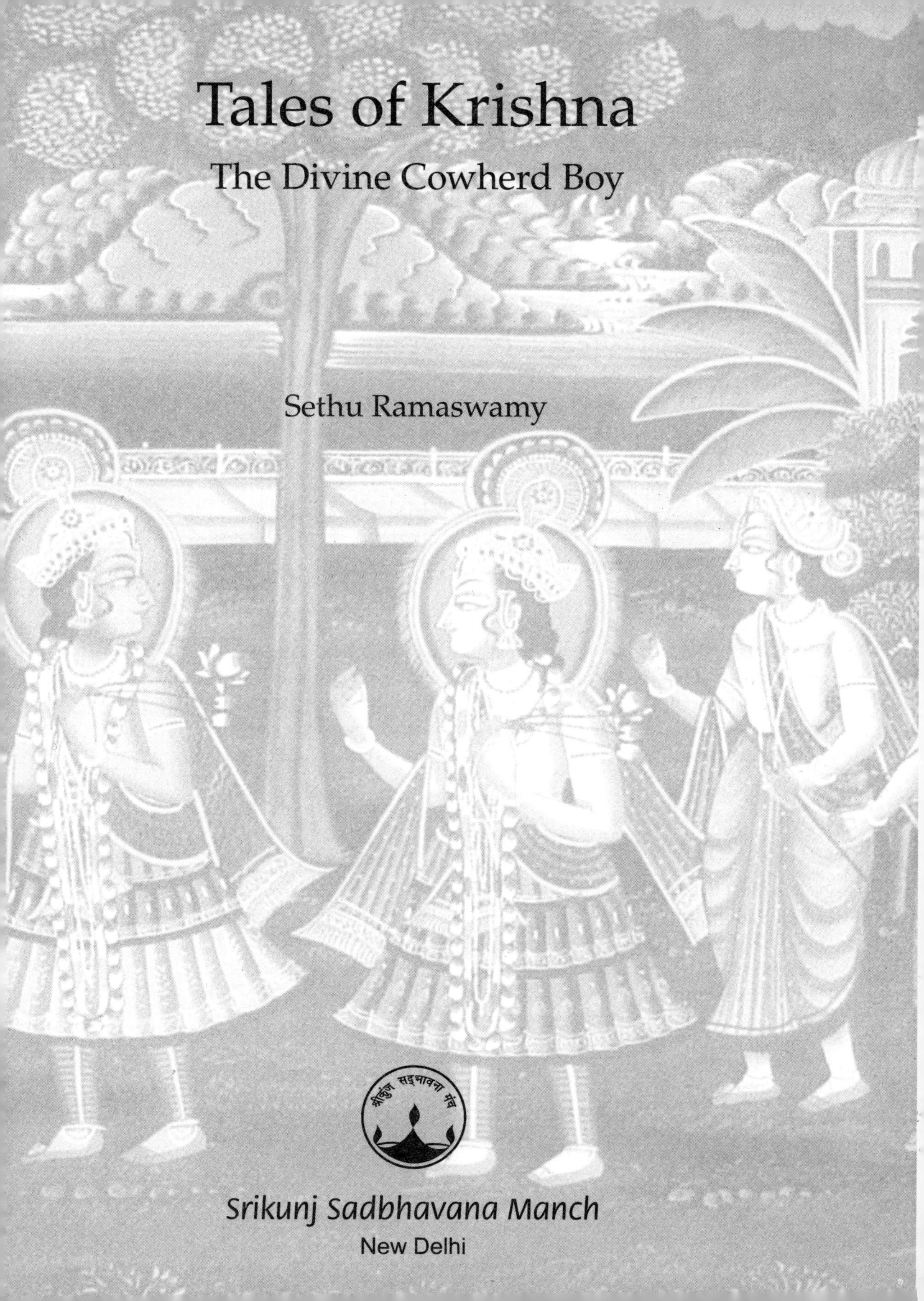

Tales of Krishna

The Divine Cowherd Boy

Sethu Ramaswamy

Srikunj Sadbhavana Manch
New Delhi

Cataloging in Publication Data — DK
[Courtesy: D.K. Agencies (P) Ltd. <docinfo@dkagencies.com>]

Ramaswamy, Sethu, 1924-
Tales of Krishna: the divine cowherd boy / Sethu Ramaswamy.
p. cm.
ISBN 13: 9788182650190
ISBN 10: 8182650194

1. Krishna (Hindu deity) 2. Hindu mythology.
I. Title.

DDC 294.5211 22

First published in India in 2012

ISBN 13: 978-81-8265-019-0 ISBN 10: 81-8265-019-4

Published and printed by:
Srikunj Sadbhavana Manch
'Srikunj', F-52, Bali Nagar
New Delhi - 110 015
Ph.: (011) 2543 3819

Distributed by:
D.K. Printworld (P) Ltd.
Regd. office : *'Vedaśrī'*, F - 395, Sudarshan Park
(Metro Station: Ramesh Nagar)
New Delhi – 110 015
Phones : (011) 2545 3975; 2546 6019; *Fax* : (011) 2546 5926
E-mail: indology@dkprintworld.com
Web: www.dkprintworld.com

To
my youngest grandson
Vijaya Krishna Ram,

and my great-grand children
Dakshina, Manisha Kiran,
Katya, Jenya, Saranya,
Ananya, Arya,

and the youngest great-grandson
Aran

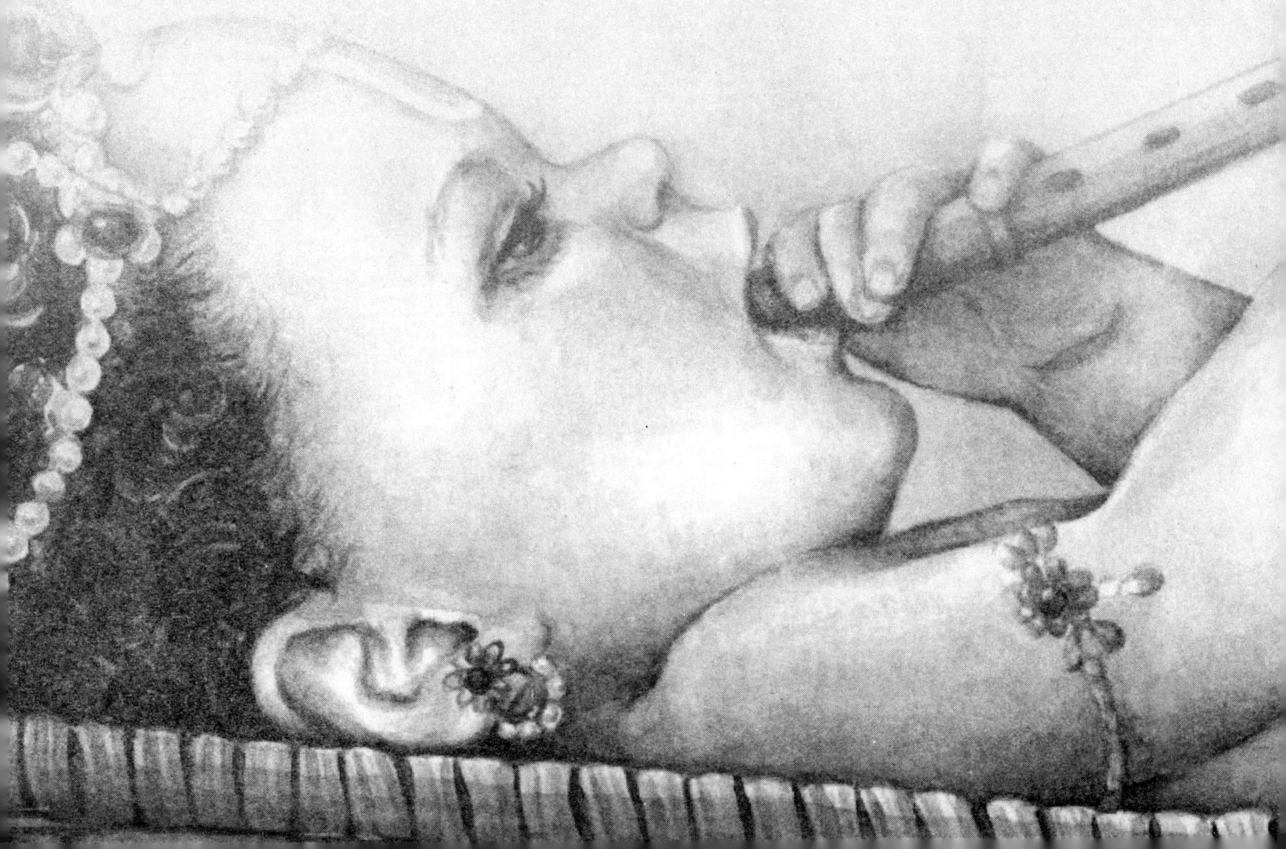

Acknowledgements

This book was written at the instance and in fact the insistence, of Sri. K.V.N. Iyengar, who had wanted me to write the tales of Krishna, the divine cowherd, in a simple, captivating style, for the young children who called him "Thaatha" and his wife "Jaya Patti." To him my warm thanks.

My blessings and thanks to my grand-daughter Divya who copy-edited the manuscripts making the much needed corrections in grammar and syntax while keeping in mind my constant plea that she should not tamper with my narrative style.

Last but not least, I would like to thank my youngest daughter Vijaya who, as always, whetted and polished the Mss, making it print-worthy.

My grateful thanks to Mr. Susheel Mittal of D.K. Printworld for bringing out the book beautifully and at the right time, as always.

New Delhi, **Sethu Ramaswamy**

31 July 2011

Contents

Introduction

King Parikshit was the son of Abhimanyu, Arjuna's son. In the *Mahabharata* Arjuna lost his beloved son Abhimanyu in the battle of Kurukshetra.

Abhimanyu was married to Uttara. Uttara was carrying Abhimanyu's child in her womb when her husband was killed in battle. The Lord protected the child in the womb of Uttara, and Parikshit was born.

Parikshit was the only surviving member of the Pandavas. He ruled the

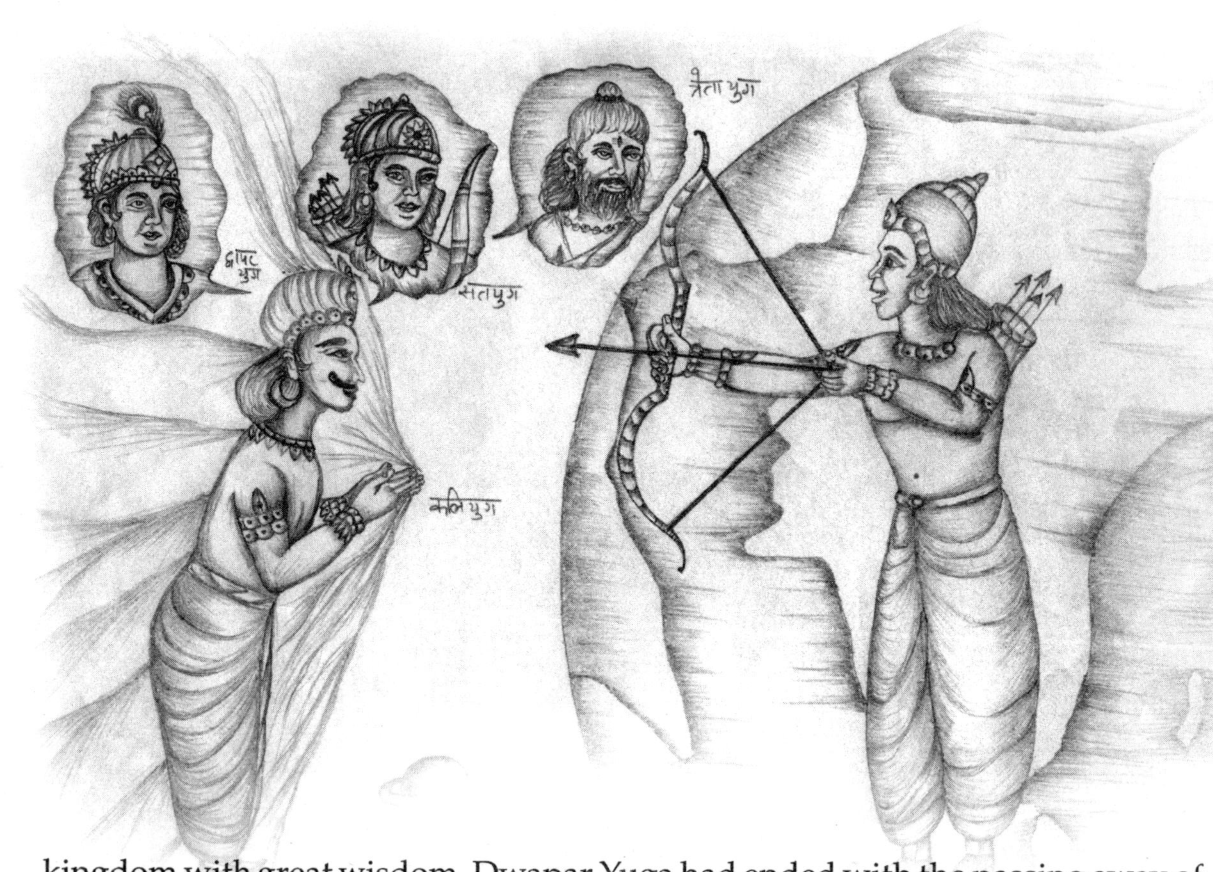

kingdom with great wisdom. Dwapar Yuga had ended with the passing away of Krishna, the *avatara* of Lord Narayana in Dwapar Yuga. Kali Yuga had begun with the advent of Kali.

In a conversation between King Parikshit and Kali Purusha, King Parikshit tells Kali, "You have no place in this land of mine, because of your association with unrighteousness (*adharma*). Here people are devoted to the Lord and to the performance of *yajnas* and to all other actions that are said to be good. Above all, they are pious, good and god-fearing, and they willingly acknowledge and adore the almighty." Kali Purusha then requested the king "show me a place where I may reign." The king replied "where there is deceit, liquor, lust, cruelty there you shall take your abode. Also where there is greed and a longing for material wealth, there you shall be."

King Parikshit had married Iravati, daughter of Uttiran, and by her was born

Janamejaya and three others. One day king Parikshit went out hunting in the forest. After some time he felt very hungry, tired and thirsty. He came to the hermitage of the great sage Shamika. The sage was in deep meditation, and could not be disturbed by Parikshit's efforts to wake him up for some water to drink. The king in frustration took up a dead snake, which was lying nearby, and threw it round the sage's neck. Even so he did not come out of his trance.

Sage Shamika's son Shringi heard that someone had thrown a dead snake on his father's neck; he cursed the person who did that by declaring that on the seventh day from then, he will be bitten by the snake Daksha and will die. When sage Shamika awoke he was angry with his son for cursing a great king like Parikshit. King Parikshit came to know of the curse and renouncing his kingdom, went on a fast unto death. He had only seven days to live.

The sage Shuka Brahmam was only a sixteen-year-old boy, an *avadhuta* (naked), his body covered by his matted locks.

Sage Shuka narrated the *Bhagavata Purana* in seven days (*Bhagavata-saptaha*) to King Parikshit so that his mind will be fixed on the Lord.

The stories on Krishna are from the *Bhagavata Purana*. Shuka had learnt it from his father Vyasa. After seven days King Parikshit was bitten by the snake Daksha and died.

1

Bhoomadevi's Sorrow

Brahma, the Lord of creation, was sitting in his celestial palace in heaven, when he heard a plaintive voice cry *amma*. The four-faced Brahma looked up from his work and found a white cow standing before him with tears flowing from her eyes. Brahma knew it was mother Earth who stood before him in the form of a cow and his heart melted with pity for the mother who was a monument of patience and bore her burdens uncomplainingly. "Why is Bhoomadevi so sorrowful? What has happened to bring her to me?" thought Brahma. He asked mother Bhooma-devi the cause of her sorrow. Mother Earth poured out her troubles — the earth was infested with cruel, wicked kings who subjected innocent people and learned sages to untold sufferings.

People were afraid to venture out for fear of being killed or arrested. Treta Yuga of Lord Rama and the reign of the Suryavamshis which had been a glorious reign had ended. In its place a reign of terror by *asuras* like Kansa had broken out, "please save me" cried Bhoomadevi.

Brahma explained to her that he could do nothing in the matter as his duty was only to create and neither could Shiva who was the destroyer. The only one who could save humanity was Vishnu — Lord Narayana the Protector, "Let us now go to Kailasa and inform Lord Parameshvara (Shiva) and take him with us to Lord Narayana who resides in the Milky Ocean in Vaikuntha" said Brahma to Bhoomadevi.

Lord Parameshvara readily agreed to go with them. A host of other gods also joined them in seeking help from Lord Narayana.

Lord Narayana was reclining and resting on Adishesha, the five-hooded serpent, with his consort Lakshmi sitting at his feet. Everyone waited with bated breath for him to wake up. But to the amazement of all a voice spoke assuring them that the time had come for Dwapar Yuga, and that Lord Narayana himself would be born on earth in the Yadava tribe to alleviate the sufferings of the people and punish the wicked. The voice also asked all the gods except Shiva and Brahma to take birth as Yadavas on earth.

Suddenly everyone disappeared from there; only Shiva, Brahma and Bhoomadevi were left. Shiva and Brahma went back to their abodes and

Bhoomadevi went back to earth happy that all her troubles would soon come to an end.

Mathura was ruled by the Yadukula kings. Prince Vasudeva, the son of King Shurasena, was to be crowned King of Mathura. Along with the coronation his marriage was fixed with the Bhoja Princess Devaki. Devaki's father was King Ugrasena, and she had an elder brother named Kansa. Kansa loved his sister Devaki very much and wanted to drive the chariot in which Devaki and her husband would go to Mathura. Her dowry was immense consisting of 400 elephants caparisoned with gold trappings, 10,000 white horses, 600 magnificent carriages, hundreds of beautiful serving maids and many other costly gifts.

Devaki was travelling with her husband Vasudeva in the chariot driven by her brother Kansa. Devaki was full of love for him as leaving all his work Kansa was driving their carriage to take her to her new home.

Kansa was fearful in appearance, a huge figure with no grace whatsoever, so it was a wonder to everyone how he was so gentle and loving to his sister Devaki. But this was when fate intervened. Suddenly the air was rent with a loud voice saying "Kansa! You are happy and proud to escort your sister to her new home in Mathura. O! fool that you are how can you know that this beloved sister of yours is going to be the cause of your death! The eighth son born to her will be your enemy and you will die at his hands. This is certain." Kansa looked at the heavens but the voice had no form and with a derisive laugh the voice ceased. Kansa stopped the chariot and got down, his face was livid with anger and his eyes became bloodshot. The caparisoned elephants, the white horses and all the accompanying carriages came to a halt.

Devaki from inside the carriage asked in her sweet voice "brother, why have you stopped? What has happened?" Was the voice from heaven heard only by Kansa? So it seemed. Vasudeva asked his brother-in-law, "What has caused you to stop the carriage? What has happened to provoke you to such anger?"

Kansa gave no reply but drew his sword and jumping into the chariot pulled his sister Devaki by her hair and raised his sword to chop off her head. Devaki cried out in anguish "brother, what are you doing? Why do you want to kill me?" Vasudeva said, "you are forgetting yourself in your anger, and are about to commit a great sin."

Then Kansa told them about the prophecy from the voice, and said, "If I do not kill this woman now, the eighth child she bears will be the death of me," and again he raised his sword. Vasudeva kneeled before Kansa at his feet and said, "O Kansa! hear me calmly, and then do what you want. Spare my wife Devaki and I promise you that when our eighth child is born I will give him up to you. You belong to the illustrious Bhoja clan, if you kill your sister the sin and blame will fall upon you. Now it is up to you to do what you want," saying this Vasudeva waited with folded hands for the verdict.

Vasudeva's plea must have moved him because Kansa told them "go now, but when your eighth child is born you must hand him over to me" and left that place.

The procession proceeded towards Mathura and

Vasudeva and Devaki reached their palace. They lived happily for some time ruling the kingdom of Mathura.

Devaki's first child was a son. Vasudeva, who was in fear of Kansa, took his son to him although Kansa had only asked for his eighth son. Kansa, seeing Vasudeva bringing his son to him, gave a loud laugh and told him "Vasudeva! You need not bring me your seven children. I want only your eighth son who is my enemy, so take your son and go back."

Vasudeva was surprised that the wicked Kansa could show such mercy. But little did he know then that Kansa would soon change his mind and kill all the six sons born to Devaki in the coming years. And that is what happened. Under evil advice Kansa decided not to take any risk and so killed the six sons of Devaki in a most cruel manner, dashing them against a stone.

One day the great sage Narada came to visit Kansa. When Narada Muni visits anyone it is with a purpose. He was known to be

a mischief-maker, but in truth all the trouble that he created ended in the triumph of good over evil.

Kansa welcomed sage Narada with great reverence. While they were discussing various matters Narada introduced the purpose of his visit. Narada began by saying "the matter which I am now going to tell you is a very great secret, but since it affects you I want to tell you so that you can be warned of the impending peril.

> The Yadava *kula* cowherds are not common people; they are all gods who have come down to earth and inhabit Gokul as ordinary cowherds. In your last birth you were an *asura*, but because of your good deeds you are now born in the illustrious royal family of the Bhojas. Now listen carefully to me.

Continued Narada:

> Lord Narayana, who is the protector of the good and destroyer of the evil-doers, will be born on this earth as the eighth child of Devaki and Vasudeva. Your *asura* nature from your previous birth will make you do evil deeds. Lord Narayana and the gods will fight you and you will die by the hand of the Lord. You and your *asura kula* beware of this danger.

After having laid the foundation of a great battle in the guise of a warning, Narada, whose mission had been completed, took leave of Kansa and left.

Kansa, instead of heeding Narada's warning and repenting of his evil ways, became more cruel. He regretted having allowed Devaki and Vasudeva to go to Mathura and live in peace. He now wanted to find a way to bring them back to Bhoja and put them in prison. But before that he imprisoned his father, King Ugrasena, and crowned himself ruler of Bhoja. He then invited his sister and her husband with great love to visit Bhoja. Poor Devaki, not knowing it was a ruse to make them leave their kingdom and come under his power, was very happy that her brother had repented and wanted her to come to Bhoja. She and her husband left for Bhoja.

But when they reached Bhoja instead of welcoming them at the palace gates they were taken straight to the prison gates. Devaki was shocked and cried out in

anguish, "Brother, what is this? You invited us with so much love and you have perpetrated this trick on us and shut us up in prison. How can you be so cruel?" she wailed.

But Kansa was unmoved. "This is where you belong, you who are going to give birth to my enemy who is going to destroy me, this is the welcome I give to you," he thundered in a loud voice. So Devaki and Vasudeva lived their life in prison. Kansa's terrible acts of cruelty increased manifold. The cries of the suffering people rent the air. He annexed all the neighbouring kingdoms and extended his powers over them.

2

Advent of Maya

Kansa had subdued the Yadava kings — the kings of Kekaya, Kuru, Panchala and also other small kingdoms, and made them vassals under him. He unleashed a reign of terror wherever he went. The time for Lord Narayana to fulfil his promise to Bhoomadevi had come.

God called Maya, the illusive spirit who is in every breath of all living beings and revealed his plan to her and ordered her to carry it out and pave the way for him to take birth on earth. The first command was that the seventh child that was growing in the womb of Devaki should be taken to Gokul and left in the womb of Rohini who was the first

Advent of Maya

wife of Vasudeva. This was because Kansa had destroyed all the six sons born to Devaki and Vasudeva who were afraid and grieving that their seventh child also would he destroyed by him. The eighth child of Devaki and Vasudeva would be Lord Narayana himself. Now the Lord instructed Maya to take birth in the womb of Yashoda, the wife of Nandagopa of the Yadavas, at the same time as he took birth in Devaki's womb. After that Vasudeva will leave the boy born to him in Gokul beside Yashoda and bring Maya and put her beside Devaki; when Kansa comes to kill the eighth child it would be Maya and she would know what to do. Maya smiling, acceded to this plan and with the Lord's blessings went on her way to carry out his orders.

Devaki conceived her seventh child but lost it early before the full term as it had been transplanted in the womb of Rohini, Vasudeva's first wife. It was the month of Shravan (Avani in Tamil) which was from 15 August to 15 September. The child inside Devaki's womb was moving and made its presence felt. Vasudeva and Devaki knew this was the birth Kansa was waiting for. They spent sleepless nights in the fear of what would happen when the child was born. The day dawned. The star in ascendance on that day was Rohini and the eighth day after the full moon. The labour pains increased and at 12 o'clock midnight the divine child was born. When the parents saw the baby, instead of fondling it they looked with awe at the child with folded hands in wonder. As they were gazing they saw a bright light almost blinding them and heard a voice saying, "I have taken birth. Take me to Gokul to the house of Nandagopa and from there bring the child born to his wife Yashoda here, leaving me beside her." Vasudeva and Devaki bowed their heads and agreed to do so. That very moment Yashoda gave birth to a girl. It was Maya who had taken birth and the child as soon as it was born gave a gurgling laugh, Yashoda felt very proud of this beautiful child. How could she know that this was Maya and she was laughing at the tricks she was going to play on Kansa? In the morning she realized her child was a boy and not a girl.

Kansa had made elaborate arrangements to guard Vasudeva and Devaki. A 24 hour vigil was kept by the guards. The prison doors were strong iron doors and heavily bolted so that not even a fly could escape let alone human beings. Vasudeva carrying out the orders of the Lord, wrapped the newborn baby in a silk cloth and put him in a basket and taking leave of Devaki stepped out and lo! The iron doors opened to let him pass and closed behind him. All the guards were awake but were in a stupor as if drugged. Vasudeva went out of the prison and walked on to the Yamuna River to cross over to Gokul. The heavens rained but Vasudeva and the divine child didn't get wet. The swollen river subsided and gave way for Vasudeva to cross with his precious burden.

When Vasudeva reached Gokul and entered Nandagopa's palace all were asleep. He quietly put down his son near Yashoda and took her baby girl and put her in the basket and giving a last look full of love for his son, left the palace of Nandagopa with the child Maya in the basket. Yashoda was fast asleep and knew nothing of what had happened. Vasudeva returned to the prison and put the girl child beside Devaki. It was nearing dawn, the child Maya gave a lusty cry and the guards came running and as instructed by Kansa they ran to convey the news to him. "We heard the cry of a baby and have

come at once to inform Your Majesty," they said.

As soon as he heard these words Kansa jumped out of his bed, drew his sword from his side and with a fiendish shout "let me kill my enemy" he strode out. On the way Kansa encountered many obstacles which were bad omens and reached the prison. He stood beside the bed of Devaki and the newborn child with his sword held aloft to strike. Devaki held his hand and pleaded with him to spare this child, "you killed all my sons, six of them, spare this girl child please, my brother," she cried. "If you kill this child I will kill myself, I cannot bear it any longer," she wept.

But Kansa was determined and he pushed Devaki aside and shouting he said "whatever you say will not move me, I have sworn to kill every child of yours" and snatching the baby from her arms he went to his palace. Devaki lay on the floor, wailing and moaning and cursing her brother and swooned away. Kansa went to the courtyard of his palace where there was a huge stone above his head and was going to dash her against the stone when something amazing happened. There was a flash of lightning and from the skies a voice like thunder was heard. Kansa felt a terrible blow on his shoulders as if a rock had fallen on him. Kansa was stunned and looked up peering into the skies. The baby girl he had held in his hands was not there, she had flown away. As he looked up he saw a figure with eight hands clapping and laughing at him. She was surrounded by celestial beings who were showering flowers on her.

Kansa was frightened and

dazed. Maya spoke to him in a teasing tone, "O you wicked fool! A little while ago you wanted to dash me on the stone and kill me. What did I do to you? Not only you, no one can kill me, now know that there is one born to kill you. When the time comes he will put an end to your atrocities. You will be humiliated and mortified and death will come to you." When the voice ceased and Kansa looked up again, Maya was not there nor the celestial beings.

Even though Kansa was a fierce, cruel *asura*, fear touched his heart. For a moment the thought crossed his mind that because he had killed all the children born to Devaki and Vasudeva he might suffer for the cruel deeds. For the first time in his life an unknown fear gripped him, he thought he should go to Devaki and Vasudeva and beg for their forgiveness, only then could he live in peace. The thought turned to action and with tearful eyes and an agitated mind he ran to the prison where Devaki and Vasudeva were kept in confinement. He begged them to forgive him saying that he was wrong in making them undergo so much suffering. He pleaded with them that he was only the instrument through which their children met their death. "Please don't hold me responsible for their deaths; it is their fate which made me so cruel. I will hereafter never cause you any suffering." Kansa showed so much remorse for his cruel deeds and spoke with so much repentance that Devaki's heart melted. Was it the wicked Kansa who is speaking like this? Has he really changed? Devaki and Vasudeva couldn't believe it, but his earnestness convinced them.

Devaki was ready to forgive him and consoled him, "brother, it does not matter. No one can escape one's fate. Perhaps we were destined to go through all that terrible suffering; our fate used you as an instrument, no blame attaches to you." Hearing her words Kansa's fears of retribution were allayed and he went back with a calm mind. Devaki and Vasudeva were released from prison, and for some time lived peacefully without anyone troubling them.

3

Krishna in Gokul

As time passed the fear of death by the hands of a boy growing up somewhere haunted Kansa and he spent sleepless nights. The words of the baby girl kept ringing in his ears. "Who is this boy who is born and growing up somewhere who is going to kill me?" — his mind kept on asking. He looked with suspicion at all the boys in his kingdom. Then the news came that a boy was born to Nandagopa of Gokul.

Everyone was talking about this handsome, charming son of Yashoda and Nandagopa. Rumours were afloat that after the birth of the boy, Gokul had good seasonal rains, the crops were plentiful and the Yadavas of Gokul were prosperous and happy. These rumours reached Kansa's ears. "There must be something divine about this child," he thought, "could he be the one to kill me?"

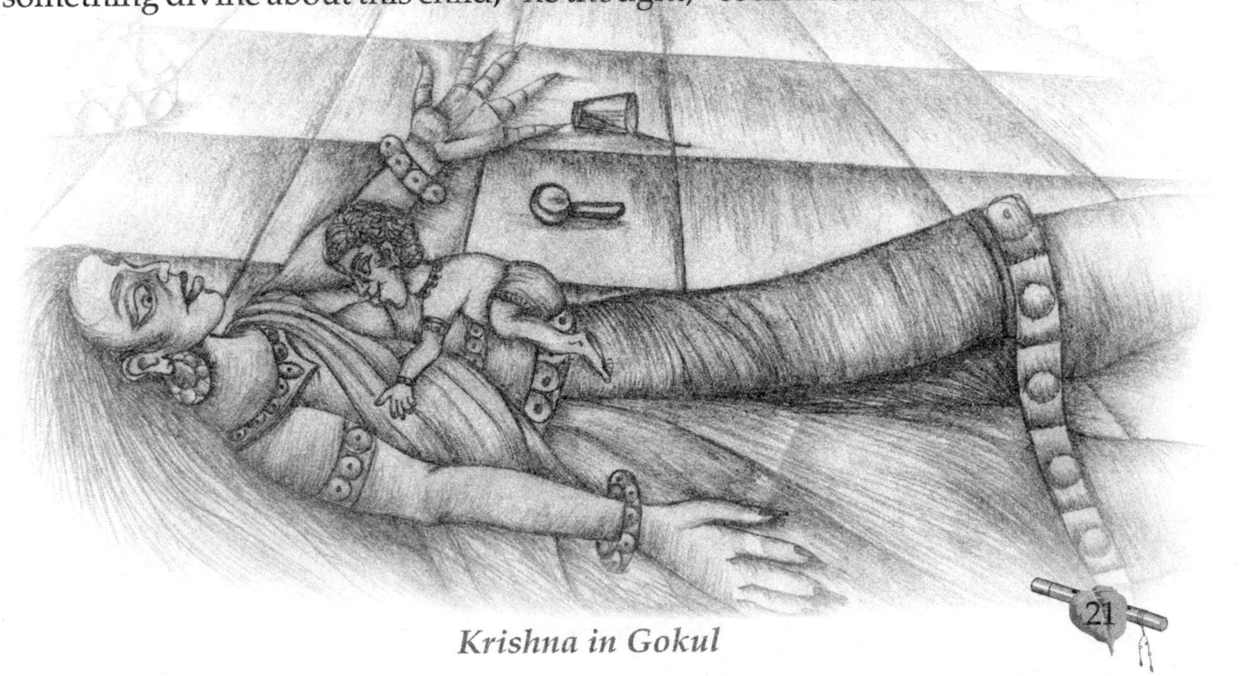

Krishna in Gokul

Why speculate, I must kill this wonder boy of Gokul. But Nandagopa should not know that I planned his death" were the thoughts that passed through Kansa's mind, and he made a plan.

The Demoness Putana

In King Kansa's kingdom there was a demoness called "Putana." Every limb and pore in her body was poisonous — she was such a cruel *rakshasi*. Kansa called for her and after explaining his plans and intention he sent her to Gokul.

Putana, as she entered Gokul, changed her fearsome appearance and went as a beautiful young woman. Seeing a beautiful damsel with a swinging gait enter the city, the guards allowed her to pass and, without any hindrance, she reached the palace of Nandagopa.

She saw Nandagopa's son playing in the front porch, he was alone, there was no one anywhere around. The child would crawl, try to stand up, walk a few steps and fall down laughing. It seemed as if he was waiting for Putana alone without anyone around. Putana ran to the beautiful boy and gathering him in her arms kissed him, fondled him, sat down and put the child to her breast. The child put his mouth to her breast and sucked the poisonous milk. Slowly as the boy's milk teeth cut into her breast, this brought an agonizing cry from the demoness, "let go, let go" she shouted, but the child's teeth on her breast only tightened. He was not sucking breast milk but her life. Putana sank down lifeless and she became her original fearful form. The boy got up and looking at the lifeless form clapped his hands in glee.

Hearing some noise Nandagopa, Yashoda and some other women came running to where the boy stood gazing at Putana with large innocent eyes. Nandagopa thought the child would have taken fright and chanted some *mantras* to calm him. Yashoda bathed him and put him in his cradle and sang soothing songs to lull him to sleep.

The huge body of the demoness was carried by the servants and cremated. Thus the demoness sent by Kansa to kill Nandagopa's son was killed by him.

Two Asuras

CHAKRASURA

Kansa came to know about the death of Putana and more alarming news was the fact that even after sucking poisonous milk of Putana the boy was hale and hearty. His suspicion about this boy being his enemy who would kill him was strengthened. The child was the son of Nandagopa and Kansa was determined to kill him. His second attempt was to send for the *asura* (demon) named Chakrasura. Kansa commanded him to go to Gokul and kill the son of Nandagopa. Thus sent by Kansa, Chakrasura came to Gokul.

The day he came there, was an important day — it was Nandagopa's son's birthday. The whole of Gokul wore a festive look. Yashoda gave her son a bath with perfumed water, and dressed him up in silk. She adorned him with jewels and put golden anklets with bells on his ankles which tinkled when he walked.

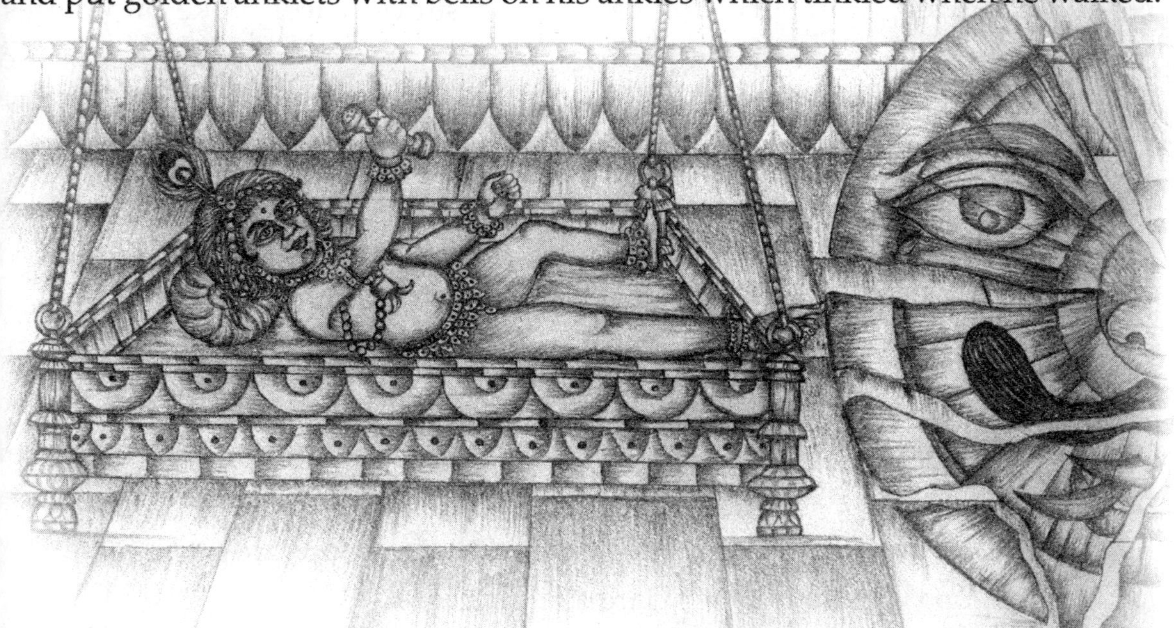

Having fed him with milk and honey, Yashoda put her son in the cradle. The cradle was decorated with sweet-smelling flowers, and the child lay there shaking his legs and hands happily.

At that time the *asura* Chakrasura sent by Kansa came there. Chakra means wheel, since he came like a wheel whose spokes were made of gold and silver and sparkled when it came rotating. The wheel went round and round the cradle Chakrasura was under the impression that the child was sleeping. His plan was to overturn the cradle and crush the boy with the weight of his wheel. The child in the cradle was fully aware of what was happening and was only pretending to be asleep. Only the tiny feet of the child were visible outside the cradle. When the *asura* Chakrasura approached the cradle to topple it, the tiny feet outside the cradle gave a kick on the wheel and stopped it.

The *asura* was taken aback. "What is this? The feet of this little child are so small that these can be held inside a palm and he has the audacity to kick me," he thought. Chakrasura redoubled his efforts and hit harder against the cradle to overturn it. There was a beatific smile on the child's face. He stretched his small feet further outside the cradle and kicked the edge of the wheel. How could there be so much strength in such tiny feet! Chakrasura's wheel broke into pieces. Some children who were playing nearby came and saw this amazing sight and were wonderstruck. Hearing the terrific noise of the wheel breaking, Nandagopa rushed into the room. Yashoda and others too came running. They found a massive wheel lying broken into pieces. Nandagopa asked the children "What happened?" The children told them that the child from the cradle kicked the wheel with his feet. But no one believed them. How could such a huge wheel get into the palace? They wondered! "Can the tiny feet of this child destroy such a huge wheel?" they asked themselves." No, no it must be some evil spirit which has possessed our son, or perhaps it must be some evil ghost that has got hold of him. Some days ago we found a demoness lying dead beside our son; today a huge wheel is lying broken. Who knows what other mishaps are going to come?" said Nandagopa with anxiety writ large on his face.

The next day he arranged for learned sages and tantrics to come and perform rituals to ward off evil spirits and tie protective *talismans* on the child's arms. He also decreed that henceforth Yashoda or the servant-maids should always be with the boy and he should never be left alone.

For some days everything was peaceful. One day Yashoda had her son on her lap and was petting him with endearing words. Suddenly she felt the child to be very heavy; it was as if a ton of iron was put on her lap. With great difficulty she put the boy down. She could not understand why he was so heavy. "Has the boy been afflicted with some dreaded disease?" she wailed. She got up and went out to fetch some old, experienced woman who could know what to do.

Taking advantage of her absence an *asura* named Trinavartta came near the child. A huge giant, he raised a lot of dust from the ground as he strode heavily towards the child. Because of the dust he raised, the world became dark; nothing was visible because of the thick haze. The whole of Gokul was dark, people stood or sat where they were, without moving. After creating the darkness, the *asura* lifted the child and flew away. Yashoda and the other women holding out their hands inched their way to the place where the child was lying, but could not lay hands on the child, as the *asura* had taken him away.

Meanwhile, Trinavartta was flying high in the clouds tightly holding the child to his chest with its arms round his neck. Suddenly, the demon found his body becoming heavy and some strong force like a mountain pushing him down. His eyes bulged out and his tongue was hanging out, and the giant *asura* was losing his balance. The child who was light when he first carried him now became so heavy. Trinavartta began to tremble with fear, "let me save myself, I don't care what happens to the child," he thought and tried to get rid of the burden he was carrying. But the child tightened his grip on the neck of the *asura*.

There was a huge thud and the *asura* crashed down on a rock near Nandagopa's house and was smashed to smithereens. Nandagopa's son was sitting on the remains of the *asura*'s dead body and laughing happily. The darkness that had engulfed Gokul disappeared and there was light. Nandagopa and Yashoda could see their son sitting on the rock. The *gopi*s (milkmaids) carried the child to Yashoda; when they saw that no harm had come to their darling boy everyone in Gokul heaved a sigh of relief and were very happy.

Everywhere the news spread about the dangers which the boy faced and how he came out unscathed from every encounter. The people talked among themselves that Nandagopa's son must be a divine child to have faced so many dangers to his life and come out safe and unharmed.

Naming the Child

The real parents of the boy who was growing up in Gokul, Devaki and Vasudeva, were very happy to know that their son was growing up well and were proud of the praises showered on him by the people who came from Gokul and gave them news about him. But they could not understand why Nandagopa and Yashoda had not yet given him a name by performing his *namakarana*. They sent word to Gargeya Muni to come to their palace. Gargeya Muni was said to be a very learned and knowledgeable scholar. They welcomed him and requested him to go to Gokul and pay a visit to Nandagopa's house where a boy was growing up and give him a suitable name. Gargeya Muni was very glad to do this as he had heard of the divine child of Nandagopa, and of his beauty and the wondrous deeds of his.

Gargeya Muni went to Gokul. Nandagopa and all the people of Gokul came out to welcome him. As a great sage had come Nandagopa took this opportunity to ask him to choose a name for their son and also perform the *namakarana* for the son of Rohini. Gargeya Muni looked into the dates of birth, month and star and planetary positions of both the children and decided on the name Balarama for Rohini's son and named Nandagopa's son Krishna. He also suggested that Balarama could also be called Rama and Krishna could also be called Vasudeva. The *gopala*s (cowherds) and *gopi*s (milkmaids) of Gokul called him affectionately "Kanha."

Balarama and Krishna grew up together. They were now boys with all portents of mischief and pranks of boys of that age. Krishna was the leader of all the boys in the neighbourhood. The *gopi*s who milked the cows and made butter and curds were his target. Although Krishna with his friends teased them and made them angry, one look at his charming face and dancing eyes would make their hearts melt with love for him. He was a source of trouble and also delight to the people of Gokul.

Kanha and his elder brother Balarama and the other cowherds of their age were supposed to take the cattle for grazing in the grassy hills or the green land near the river banks, and bring them home in the evening. But Kanha's mind and heart was bent more upon mischief than work.

4

Krishna's Pranks

The Thief Who Stole Butter

The *gopis* had to get up early and milk the cows. They would first let the calves feed from their mothers and then they would be tied to the fence and the *gopis* would come to milk the cows one by one. Krishna would silently creep up to where the calves were tied and let them loose. The calves would naturally run to their mothers and drink milk to their full, and romp round the house. How did the calves break away and come? asked the people who were in the house to no one in particular, first expressing their wonder. Krishna would stand in front of them and clapping his hands laugh gleefully. That day there would be no milk from the cows.

In the houses of the *gopis* the curds and butter were kept high in earthen pots inside rope baskets hanging from the roof. When the womenfolk had gone to the river to bathe, Krishna would lead his brigade and enter a *gopi's* house. He would make one boy bend and the others one by one would climb on each other bending till Krishna reached the top and could take the butter or curds from the pot which was kept inside the rope basket. He would bring it down and distribute it to all his friends and manage to consume quite a major portion himself. After having emptied the pots they would leave the pots under a tree where there were monkeys and call the *gopis* and show them the pots which the monkeys would be tossing about, and blatantly lie that the monkeys had come to their houses and taken the pots and eaten up the contents, and are now playing with the pots. All this Krishna would say, his face full of mirth.

Sometimes Krishna would collect stones and pelt them at the pot containing milk or curds and when he made a hole he would cup his heads and drink his fill. If he was caught by anyone while stealing curds or butter he would stuff their mouths with the remaining butter or curds and run away. There was no limit to the pranks of this divine child throughout Gokul.

One day he was caught red-handed by some *gopis* and they dragged him with them to Yashoda to complain about him "at last we caught the butter thief" they exulted and were happily going to his house to see him punished, but as they neared his house Krishna suddenly vanished. They couldn't find him anywhere when they reached Yashoda's house to tell her about him, they found her giving him a bath and Krishna looked at them with an innocent look on his face though his eyes were twinkling. They couldn't believe or comprehend how he could get away from them and be bathing here.

One must understand that Krishna or Kanha as the people of Gokul affectionately called him was only playing these pranks, like stealing butter and teasing the *gopis* only to show that he was an ordinary child, mischievous and playful.

Yashoda Sees the Universe

Another time something great happened. Kanha was playing with friends of his own age, when he started eating the soft mud filling his mouth with it and swallowing with relish. They all went running to Yashoda and said talking all together "your son is eating mud, we told him not to eat but he wouldn't listen."

Yashoda came running out, crying "Oh! What will happen? He will get an infection of the stomach. What will I do?" She asked him to open his mouth wide to take out the mud, but stood petrified. She saw in his wide mouth all the oceans, mountains, the sky, the sun and moon — the whole universe — including Gokul, Krishna and Yashoda herself.

Kanha closed his mouth. Yashoda gathered her son in her arms; she forgot he was her son, born to her. She only knew he was God, otherwise how could she see the universe in his small mouth. "He is not an ordinary child, he was divine. He was not born to be my child alone, he belonged not only to Gokul but to the whole world and he has come to do great deeds to save the world." All these thoughts flooded her mind. She told Nandagopa and the others in Gokul about this strange miracle.

Nandagopa was also overwhelmed by the signs of divinity he found in his son's action. He told Yashoda "Yashoda, this son of ours is born in this world for a purpose. His mischievous pranks and playfulness are only to make us forget his divinity. Wait and see what great deeds this son of ours, Krishna, is going to do."

Nala Purush

One day Yashoda was busy in the kitchen. Krishna was also busy trying to open the big pot in which Yashoda had kept thick creamy curds. He looked here and there furtively and put both his hands right into the pot and was busy eating the curds. His whole body was smeared with curd. To hold the pot firmly, he held it between his two feet and with his hands scooped out the curds, his body bent over the pot, and the curds poured out all over the floor making a pool. Hearing the noise of something breaking, Yashoda came running from the kitchen and found Kanha standing in the middle of the pool of curds, himself covered with curds. Yashoda became furious and picking a stick came to give Krishna a thrashing. Did she expect Krishna to wait for her to beat him, as soon as he saw his mother coming he took to his heels and ran as fast as his little legs would take him. Yashoda ran after him with the stick but Kanha ran faster and she could not catch up with him. She was getting tired and breathless when Krishna suddenly stopped and allowed himself to be caught. Yes, he couldn't bear to see his dear mother tired so he gave himself up, not because he was tired of running. Yashoda held her son by his hands and raised her stick to beat him, but she couldn't; she saw the laughing, sweet face of her darling son and dropped the stick. But the boy must be punished, it is a mother's duty, so she thought of another way of punishing him without beating him.

She took Krishna to the courtyard in the centre of the house and tied him to a pounding stone. Did Yashoda forget his divinity? Did she forget the miracle of seeing the universe in his tiny mouth? She remembered nothing of all that and wanted to tie up this divine being to a stone. Krishna wanted to have some fun with his sweet mother. Yashoda had brought a good length of rope sufficient to go round the pounding stone two or three times. What is this? How can this happen? Yashoda was astounded. This little boy couldn't be tied with even such a long length of rope! She went and brought another long rope knotted it with the previous one and tied Krishna round the waist taking the rope several times round his body. Even so she couldn't tie him, the rope fell loose.

Yashoda did not know what to do. "I am not able to tie up this boy" she fumed. Krishna looked at his mother and felt sorry for teasing her, he now allowed himself to be firmly tied to the pounding stone by a small length of rope. Yashoda put her finger on her nose in wonder, "Kanha, I brought so much rope to tie you, I couldn't, now you are tied firmly with a small rope, how is this?" she asked her son. Krishna, who was tied to the pounding stone, didn't answer her; instead he looked at his mother and gave an enchanting smile.

Confident that her son was securely tied and could not do mischief Yashoda went about her work. Krishna sat down near the stone for some time. How long can the playful boy be quiet? He slowly got up and dragged himself along with the heavy stone which would require four people to move, towards the edge of the courtyard. There were two trees almost the same height and thickness. The trunks of the two trees were wide and branches were spreading out. Krishna now increased his speed and almost ran to where the two trees stood. As Krishna came between the two trees the branches began to swing and dance in the breeze as he had dragged the pounding stone also with him. Although he was able to go between the trees, the stone got stuck. Krishna tried to push the trees with his feet to make the stone come through. Suddenly a tremendous ear-splitting noise rent the air as of a thousand thunderbolts. Next minute a sound like the sawing of trees was heard. Krishna closed his eyes pretending to be afraid, when he opened them both the trees had fallen down, and two handsome youths, the sons of Lord Kubera, were standing there. When they saw the child Krishna, they bowed before him with folded hands. Krishna blessed them, and their past came to his mind. They told Krishna that sage Narada had cursed them, but had also told them that they would be redeemed from the curse by Lord Narayana who would be born in Gokul as Krishna.

Why sage Narada cursed them is a separate story which is not relevant here. Let us go on with the story of Krishna and his *lila*s.

The Blackberry Seller

One day Krishna was playing with his friends in the streets of Gokul, he saw an old woman selling black-berries (*Nagapazham* or *jamun*) in exchange for grain. The children ran off to their homes and came with both their hands full of grain and gave it to the old woman. In exchange she gave them a handful of ripe black-berries. Krishna also ran to his home and from the barrel, in which grain was stored, brought grain in both his hands held closely together, but when he came there, all the grain had fallen through his fingers all the way and there were only a few grains left in his hands. He stood in front of the berry seller with tears in his

eyes and those few grains in his hands. The old woman thought "how can I sell my fruit without getting grain in return?" but when she looked at the beautiful, divine face of the child she called him and kissed his forehead and picked out the best berries from her basket and filled his hands with the fruit. Before the old woman gave him the berries Krishna shook the few grains he had, into the woman's basket. The grains that fell became gold. The old woman was wonderstruck and bent down and kissed his divine hands, and went away with love for that little boy with tears in her eyes. Krishna enjoyed the berries with his friends.

5

In Vrindavan

Krishna the Giant Killer

About this time Nandagopa and most of his relatives and friends decided to move out of Gokul to Vrindavan, as Nandagopa and Yashoda felt that too many accidents had happened to their Kanha for them to take it lightly. They feared for the safety of their precious son. They thought of Putana lying dead beside the child, then Chakrasura and Trinavartta, and who knows who else might come? For all these reasons they decided to shift to Vrindavan. The people of Gokul were enchanted by the green pastures and luscious foliage of Vrindavan. The Yamuna River flowed peacefully and the children were very happy to play on the banks of the Yamuna.

Their cows, calves and goats grazed on sweet grass. Krishna and his elder brother Balarama were now old enough to go out with the other boys to graze their cattle and bring them home safely in the evening. While their cattle grazed, the cowherd boys enjoyed themselves, swimming and bathing in the river, playing, and eating their midday food packet sitting under the shade of the spreading trees.

One day as Balarama and Krishna were out with the other cowherds grazing the cattle, Krishna noticed an unusually big male calf come close to him and brush against him. He also observed that the calf stayed close to him and would butt him. He had no memory of seeing this particular calf in Gokul among Nandagopa's flock. He became suspicious of the young bull. He knew it was not

a genuine calf but an *asura* who had taken the form of a calf only to attack him. Who would have sent it? Of that also he had an inkling, but did not want to reveal the truth now, and decided to wait for the appropriate time.

All the cows were going towards where the grass was thickest and the big calf was also moving but very close to Krishna. When they came near a huge fruit tree the big calf suddenly sprang on Krishna, but he had already anticipated this move of the *asura* and as the beast sprang he bent back and took hold of the beast's two forelegs and lifted it high and swirling it, dashed the beast against the tree causing huge branches of the tree laden with unripe and ripe fruit to fall down. The young bull's bones were broken as it lay dead. The dead body was not that of a bull but of an *asura* called Vatsasura. Kanha now knew for certain that the *asura* was sent by Kansa.

The Killing of Bakasura

It was noon and the weather was hot. The cattle were drinking water from the river and the cowherd boys were sitting in the shade of the trees nearby and eating their packed lunch of curd, rice and pickles.

Krishna alone sat further away perhaps anticipating something to happen. Sure enough what he anticipated was coming nearer to him like a huge white hill from afar. Krishna saw that the hill was a huge stork, its huge beak was wide and strong enough to swallow a whole army. When this monstrous bird flapped its wings it produced a dust storm.

The cattle which were peacefully drinking water, mooing loudly scampered away to safety. The boys having their midday lunch ran away in fright. Only Kanha stood calmly with a broad smile on his face, awaiting Bakasura. The stork came near Krishna and opened wide its beak to swallow him. Krishna kept quiet and allowed the stork to swallow him. When the other boys who were standing cried aloud "alas! The stork has eaten up our Kanha." But Krishna clung firmly to the gullet of the bird and when it tried to push him down further, the stork's long neck and gullet started burning. The stork was choking so it opened its beak and spat out Krishna who came out safe and sound. Now

not original, but created by Paramatma. Brahma was also surprised as he had hidden the cowherd boys and the cattle in a cave in the mountains. How could Krishna have brought them back? He ran to the cave where he had hidden them and found them all there. He realized the greatness of Krishna and set free all the boys and the cattle and went to Krishna and begged his forgiveness. Such great deeds were performed as if it was child's play by Krishna who smilingly forgave Brahma.

The Battle of Panangkadu

Kanha was at an age when children are prone to mischief, enjoying every moment of life, playing, dancing, singing, playing the flute, teasing the maidens and women. Krishna was always to be found with his friends playing on the banks of the Yamuna or roaming the hills and forests around Vrindavan. Many were the exploits of Krishna which ended in doing good for the people.

One day, Krishna, who was now the acknowledged leader of the cowherd boys of Gokul, was going with Balarama and his friends to the hills and forests of Vrindavan to graze their cattle. The green pastures were dotted with white cows grazing. They were called by names like Lakshmi, Sasi, Mohi, etc. — every cow had a name.

While the cows were feeding on the grass, the children were enjoying themselves, laughing, talking, shouting, chasing each other and roaming in the forest. After some time they got tired and rested themselves under the shade of a spreading tree. Balarama put his head on his younger brother Krishna's lap and slept. Krishna sat quiet not moving lest his brother should wake up.

After a good siesta Balarama woke up refreshed. They went in search of the others, and all of them gathered together.

At that time a group of people came there with anxious faces. Krishna and Balarama asked everyone to be quiet as these people seemed to be in great trouble.

They greeted Balarama and Krishna and straightaway told them their troubles. "We know you are only young boys, but we have heard about your prowess or perhaps your divine power to vanquish even wicked *asura*s. We come from a place called Panangkadu which is not far from here; there an *asura* named Dhenukasura with his tribe of *asura*s is devastating the place. We cannot graze our cattle for fear of him, nor can we farm our land. We cannot pluck fruits from our trees which are famous for its fragrant luscious fruit.

"The learned sages cannot perform their ritual worship, the people are terrified of going out, please, please we beg of you to help us and drive away those *asuras*," they pleaded. Krishna and Balarama looked at each other and smiled. They then turned to the Gokul boys and asked, "Are you prepared to fight the *asura*s and help these poor people?" At once all the cowherd boys rose

Akasura could not hold it anymore and Krishna tore the *asura*'s head apart and came out. All those who were inside the snake were unconscious because of the poison. Krishna made them all regain consciousness and they got up and came out of the snake's body.

Akasura realized that this boy Krishna was no ordinary mortal, he must be God, and bowed before Krishna asking for forgiveness.

The friends of Krishna looked in awe at this spectacle; even the cows were quiet as if sensing the greatness of Krishna.

They also realized that Krishna was not an ordinary boy like them; he had some magic in him. Till now they considered him as their friend and their equal but now they felt a great respect and love for their playmate and friend. Henceforth he became their leader and guide.

The Strange Disappearance

It was a glorious morning. The Gokul crowd of boys with their cows and calves had come to the river bank. The cattle were grazing and the boys were sitting under the shade of the trees, and taking their meals of curd-rice and pickles. Krishna and Balarama also had brought their lunch and they were all chatting and eating. Afterwards Krishna played his flute and everyone listened with rapt attention. Although nowadays they thought of him as their leader and had respect for him, Krishna just wanted to be one of them and not someone extraordinary. He made them laugh with his jokes and all were having a good time.

Suddenly they noticed the cattle had disappeared. Where could they go? What had happened? The boys were frightened and began to cry. Krishna pacified them saying "don't worry, I will bring your cows and calves just wait for me here," and Krishna went in search of the cattle.

Krishna searched for the lost cattle along the banks of the Yamuna, but could not find them. He came back to the place where his friends were but was startled to find no one there. Just as the cows and calves had disappeared, his friends also had disappeared.

Now Krishna knew it was done deliberately by someone and he knew it could only be Brahma. It was evening and very soon it would be dark. If all the cowherd boys and the cattle did not come home by evening, his parents and the other parents would get worried. A search party would be coming to the river bank. Krishna thought for a while. He then came to a decision and with his divine power he created in duplicate all the Gokul boys and all the cows and calves and they all went home.

For some days the boys and cattle created by Krishna were in Vrindavan. No one except Krishna knew that they were not the real ones.

One day a cowherd named Balabhadra was grazing his cattle with the other cowherds and the truth came out. He realized that the cowherds and cattle were

the stork was afraid of Krishna and started to run but he caught hold of its beak and tore it into two and killed it. It was Bakasura, an *asura* sent by Kansa, who lay dead on the ground.

The boys, who were watching all this, ran home shouting to everyone they met how Kanha had killed a stork who was actually the *asura* Bakasura. Nandagopa and Yashoda came running out and saw Krishna with his friends happily coming home. Nandagopa lifted his son and hugged him. They had left Gokul and come to Vrindavan to escape from Kansa's machinations but he was still sending *asura*s to trouble them. Everyone was concerned about the safety of Krishna.

Krishna Kills Akasura

The season was spring, everywhere there was greenery, flowers of all colours and hues bloomed in plenty, and Vrindavan looked enchanting.

The children of Vrindavan begged their parents to allow them to go on a picnic to the hill forest near the banks of the Yamuna. Balarama and Krishna also joined them. All of them brought delicious, packed lunch from home which they could pool and eat.

They set out early and letting the cattle graze on the fresh green grass, they went into the forest which was one riot of colours with flowers and trees laden with fruits and plucked the fruits to eat. They plucked the flowers from the trees and also picked flowers fallen on the ground and made garlands and wore them. Some garlands they rolled into a ball and played throwing the flower ball at each other. Some boys hid the lunch packs of their friends and had their boxes hidden by them, in turn.

It was all fun and play. The boys jumped into the river and splashed about, swimming. Krishna and Balarama saw some monkeys watching them and threw fruits at them which they jumped and caught and then the boys chased them away.

While they were playing, they saw creeping down from a tree a snake as fat as an elephant's leg and going towards Kanha who was standing under that very same tree. The boys shouted "snake, snake" and ran some distance away from the snake. Krishna could not run away as the snake was already upon him. He could not do anything. But Krishna was no ordinary boys. As Lord Narayana he was used to recline on the huge snake Adishesha. Krishna hid himself from the snake, but the snake in anger went to where the boys were standing and swallowed all of them. It was so huge they could not escape. The snake then swallowed all the cattle. Krishna now came out of his hiding and decided that in order to save his friends and the cows he should allow himself to be swallowed up by the snake.

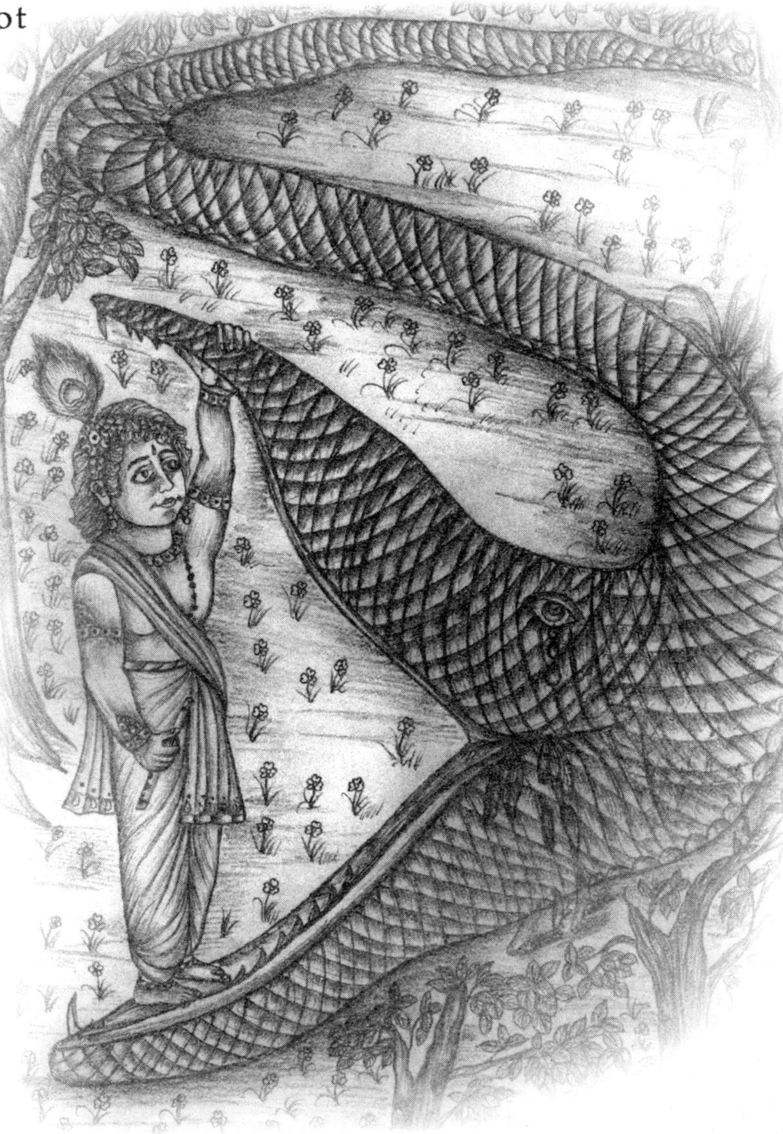

As soon as the snake saw Krishna it swallowed him. This huge snake was Akasura. Krishna knew this, and from inside the snake he made his body grow and grow and it went on expanding till

up in anger and vowed to kill Dhenukasura and his kinsmen, under the leadership of Krishna and Balarama.

They then marched as if for battle towards Panangkadu, the people who had come from there leading, showing them the way.

They reached Panangkadu forest where Dhenukasura and the other *asura*s lived, and uprooted the trees and broke the huge branches. Hearing the loud noise Dhenukasura, shouting in a thunder-like voice, came there.

As he strode, the earth shook, so massive was he. His face was long like a donkey, his body was black, his ears were long like spears, a truly repulsive form, he came towards Krishna and Balarama. Dhenukasura sprang upon Balarama and with his legs kicked him. Balarama stood quietly smiling as if he was not prepared to fight him. The second time Dhenukasura came charging with his legs to kick him, Balarama suddenly bent down and held both the legs of the *asura* and lifting him swirled him round and round his head and flung him far away. The force of the throw made Dhenukasura hit against a tall palm tree and he fell down in pieces. Everyone gave cries of joy on seeing the end of wicked Dhenukasura, but their joyous shouts were drowned by fearful cries from the other *asura*s who wanted to avenge the death of their leader Dhenukasura.

A fierce battle followed, the army of Krishna and Balarama and the Gokul boys fighting the *asura*s. The Gokul army may consist of young lads but they had stout hearts and with their Kanha as leader and Balarama, the *asura*s were soon vanquished and the dead lay scattered on the ground.

Panangkadu was now safe for the people and they could enjoy the fruits and flowers of their forest. They could live their lives in peace without fear.

It was evening and the Gokul cowherds with their cattle started on their journey home. In every house the parents of the children were waiting anxiously for them, listening for the sound of the jingling cowbells announcing their return and were happy to see their boys back. They knew that as long as Krishna and Balarama were with them they need have no fear for the safety of their boys.

The Dance of Kaliya

Yamuna, one of the tributaries of the Ganges, flowed through many territories, towns and villages. It was beneficent to all living beings — humans, animals, trees and plants. The force of the Yamuna flowing through the territories created huge ponds. In Vrindavan there were two such ponds; one was occupied by a huge snake called Kaliya, he lived there with his wives and children. He was a poisonous snake emitting poison through his tongue which would poison the atmosphere. Birds flying over the pond would inhale the poisonous air and fall dead to the ground. Trees and plants did not flourish there. No one could go near the pond and if strangers who did not know that the water was poisoned because of Kaliya, happened to quench their thirst with the water from the pond they would die. The fair name of the beautiful river Yamuna was spoilt because of Kaliya. Everyone was waiting for the day when some great saviour would kill Kaliya and save them.

Well, that saviour was soon to come. One day Krishna and his friends were playing along the banks of the Yamuna and without realizing it they came to the poisonous pond. The only tree near the pond was the Kadamba tree, and one of its branches had bent so far as to almost touch the centre of the pond where Kaliya lived.

The Gokul children stopped far away from the pond as they knew it was poisonous, but Krishna, laughing, went to the edge of the pond and climbed the Kadamba tree. The other boys from a distance shouted hoarse asking him to come back, but Krishna gestured to them to keep quiet and held on to the branch which was bent near the centre of the pond. Sitting on that branch he splashed the water with his legs, as if he wanted to bring Kaliya out.

Suddenly a big movement like waves rising was seen, the air was filled with poisonous fumes, a huge snake made his appearance from the centre of the pond. His broad hood was shining as if it was molten gold. Krishna who was sitting on the branch of the Kadamba tree jumped onto Kaliya's broad hood.

subsided till it completely disappeared. It was an automatic action for the people to turn to Krishna who was only a young boy, but they seemed to know that only he could save them. At dawn they returned to Vrindavan. Nandagopa and Yashoda and the other elders were amazed at this great deed of their son. Again the thought came to them that Krishna was born to do great deeds, and wondered what his future would be.

6

The Lilas of Krishna

Spring had come and gone and it was summer. The days were warm and people from far and near came to the banks of the river Yamuna and returned home only after the sun had set. They spent time bathing, swimming

tail-end of Kaliya and twisted it. He jumped on Kaliya's broad hood and trampled on his head, as soon as Kaliya opened his mouth to bite him. Krishna pressed his foot on that hood, and so he went on putting his foot alternately on his hoods whenever Kaliya raised his head to bite.

To the people watching from the banks of the river it looked like Krishna was dancing on Kaliya. This scene in the *Bhagavatam* is described as Kalinga Nartanam (The Kalinga dance). At first Kaliya thought "what harm can this little boy do with his little feet? It will only be like giving me a massage," but as Krishna kept on jumping on his hoods he realized the pressure on his head was becoming unbearable, and cried out in agony. As Krishna went on dancing or rather pounding on the heads of Kaliya, the snake became weak and the poison and blood flowed out from his body.

For years Kaliya had been the cause of the death of so many people, animals, birds and plants, now he was dying inch by inch painfully.

Another realization came to Kaliya at that moment; he realized his mistake in thinking that the feet pressing his head was that of a little boy. "He is not an ordinary child, he is God, my poisonous fumes and the poisonous water did not affect him. No one can destroy him, but he can destroy anyone however strong he may be. Oh! This child will kill me," he thought.

Now Kaliya's wives came up and when they saw the condition of their husband they fell at Krishna's feet and begged him to spare his life. Krishna in pity for those female snakes took his feet off from Kaliya's head. Kaliya felt as if a mountain was lifted from his head.

Krishna smiled his enchanting smile and told the snake,

> Kaliya! The river Yamuna is for people and cattle to bathe and drink water. Poisonous snakes like you should not live here. Take your tribe and go to the sea.
>
> I know that in your previous birth you were afraid of Garuda so you were hiding here. Now you no longer need fear him, as I have imprinted my feet on your head.

Kaliya went away with his wives and all the snakes to the sea.

Now the pond was safe for everyone. Krishna went to the river bank where his father and mother and the people of Gokul were waiting for him.

That evening no one returned home. It was dark and the walk was long, so they decided to sleep that night under the trees near the forest, and go back in the early dawn next day. Everyone was tired and just stretched themselves wherever there was soft grass and were sound asleep.

A Fresh Danger

The Gokul people were sleeping when suddenly they awoke smelling fire and feeling the heat, and found that a forest fire had spread round them so much that they could not cross the fire and escape. The cattle sensing the danger had run helter-skelter. All the people in one voice asked Krishna to save them.

Krishna woke up and walked along the ring of fire and as he walked, the fire

His friends who were watching Krishna with fear thought that he was caught by Kaliya and started wailing, "alas! Kaliya has caught our Kanha." Kanha gave them a triumphant smile standing on Kaliya's head; this somewhat allayed their fears.

Kaliya was swelling his body and he clenched his poisonous fangs and swished his tail and tried to kill Krishna, but Krishna stood firm as Kaliya wound his body like a rope round Krishna tightly. Those who were watching from the banks were so frightened, some swooned, some started weeping. Krishna allowed himself to be tied. When Kaliya coiled round Kanha tightly, the earth shook in anger like an earthquake.

Sparks began to fall from the sky. In the village Nandagopa and all the villagers felt a kind of fear, Nandagopa was trembling. Only Krishna's elder brother Balarama was laughing to himself. He knew that Krishna was not only playful but also courageous and he was fighting an evil snake to do good to the people.

Nandagopa with Yashoda and elders went in search of Krishna and the boys. They searched for them everywhere but could not find them. Then as they were walking along the banks of the Yamuna they came upon the cowherd boys anxiously looking at the pond. They saw their Kanha standing on Kaliya's head but the snake's coil was wound round him tightly.

When they saw Krishna in this plight they all cried aloud wailing "alas! Kaliya has Kanha in his coils, is there no one here to save him?" Krishna could see his father and others crying and wringing their hands anxiously, but kept quiet and pretended not to have seen them. All of them were shouting "Kanha, Kanha, is this your fate that you should die like this? How can we bear it?" they wailed. At last Krishna relented and by his powers expanded his body. As he grew bigger Kaliya was shrinking and he wilted, his whole head was bulging out, he could not breathe. Krishna now was a huge form and the coils of the snake round him were breaking and Krishna became free. Now Kaliya could not hold Krishna so he wanted to kill him by emitting poisonous fumes. The poisonous fumes were thick and were spreading, even those who were far away on the river bank were choking and moved still farther away.

Till now Krishna had been patient, but now he became angry and pulled the

and staying in the water till their bodies were cool. Then they had their packed lunch under the shade of the spreading trees of the forest, where the cool breeze from the river fanned them.

These were like festive days, with groups of people chatting and laughing and enjoying themselves. Among them were Krishna, Balarama and their friends.

All the unmarried *gopis* had their eyes on Krishna, and were whispering among themselves and praising his beautiful eyes and charming face. Some *gopis* expressed the opinion that it was his curls which fell over his forehead that made him look so enchanting, stole glances at him and declared it was his mouth with red lips that made him so beautiful and so on.

They stole glances at him and when he looked their way they would pretend they were looking at something else.

Krishna would take out his flute and, leaning against a tree with his legs crossed, would close his eyes and play a tune.

The music would draw the attention of everyone and they would sit still listening to the melody that flowed from his lips. Even the cows and calves would stay still and listen not even chewing the cud. The *gopikas* would listen with rapt attention swaying to the music. Abruptly he would stop and the *gopis* would crowd round him begging him to continue. Sometimes he would, sometimes he wouldn't, wasn't he the mischievous Kanha?

Thus the summer months went by and the days were getting cold. Now very few people came to the river.

The Katyayani Vrata

The unmarried *gopis* of Gokul and Vrindavan were observing a *vrata* (ritual fast) during the month of Margashirsha (15 December to 15 January) and they came to the river in the early hours before it dawned and the sun rose, and had their bath in the river. After bathing they wore beautiful *sarees* and decked themselves with flowers on the wet hair, blackened their eyes with collyrium, and put the red vermilion on the centre of their foreheads.

They poured water from a mug on mud and moulded it into a tall mound, which represented the goddess Katyayani. They decorated Devi with flower garlands, applied vemilion, turmeric and sandalwood paste and performed *puja*. This *vrata* was for granting them good husbands. All the thirty days of the month they should religiously observe this fast and perform *puja*, they had food only once at night. They would get up very early and knock on the door of their

friends to wake them up and all of them would reach the river before dawn.

Krishna knew about the *vrata* and had seen the pretty *gopi*s go in a group to the river in the early dawn. He wanted to tease them and one day he and his friends went ahead of them to the river bank and were waiting for them. Kanha hid himself in the bushes near the bank where the *gopi*s would come for their bath and asked the other boys to hide somewhere further away. He had stationed himself at a vantage point from where he could see the *gopi*s bathing. They came laughing and talking to the river bank.

The *gopi*s removed all their clothes and got into the water. As it was dark no one could see them, so they thought they were safe and could enjoy their bath more in the nude. But that day they did not know that a pair of black eyes was watching them from a tree. Leaving their clothes piled up on the bank they immersed themselves in the cold water, screaming as the chill water touched their bodies.

Krishna noiselessly crept up to where they were bathing and watched them stealthily. He stood there in the dark seeing them frolicking and splashing water on each other. His eyes were dancing with mischief as he quietly took away all their clothes and climbed up a tree overlooking the river. He hung all the clothes on the branches of the tree. Then he made a noise as of clearing his throat to attract their attention.

When the *gopi*s heard a noise coming from the tree they looked up and peered intensely to see who it was, and saw a small figure and knew it was Kanha as he was laughing away. They felt so ashamed that they immersed themselves again in the water.

Slowly they surfaced only showing their heads, shrinking and blushing with shame they begged Kanha to give them back their clothes. "Kanha! What do you gain by teasing us? How can you subject us to this shameful plight? Please give us our clothes back," one of them pleaded. Another *gopi* with tears in her eyes spoke to Krishna thus: "O, darling of Gokul! You are a good, sweet boy; please give us back our clothes." At once all the *gopis* cried out loud in one voice and forgetting their shame raised their hands folded in a prayerful attitude. Hearing their individual and collective appeals Krishna laughed. He then asked them, "you *gopis*! All of you are undertaking this *vrata*, isn't it? Whom are you thinking of when you pray? I know in your mind the husband you all want to marry. If you all want to marry the same person, how is it possible? Who will get that one person?" All the *gopis* hung down their heads in embarrassment.

Krishna then said "O Lovely maidens! I have no intention or desire to insult your modesty or put you to shame. I only wanted to test you, and expose the wrong purpose of your *vrata*, which is asking for the impossible." So saying he gave them back their clothes. They wrapped their *sarees* round themselves and bowing before Kanha they went home.

The Test of Devotion

In a forest near Vrindavan some *rishi*s were performing an important ritual worship — a *yajna* for several days, in order to obtain the grace of Lord Narayana. Krishna came to know of this and it occurred to him to test the true devotion of the *rishi*s (sages) who were performing the *yajna*.

He called his Gokul friends and told them "go to the nearby forest where some *rishi*s are performing a *yajna*, and tell them that you are hungry and starving and ask them for food. If they ask you who you are you must reply that you are known to Krishna and Balarama and that it was they who sent you," and Krishna sent them on their way.

The Gokul cowherd boys went to the place where the *rishi*s were performing the *yajna*, and told them that they were very hungry and starving, and that Krishna and Balarama had sent them here. "Please give us food, we are starving" they asked the *rishi*s. The boys saw that a huge amount of food was kept ready, but the *rishi*s were not willing to feed the hungry boys, and did not care to look at them or talk to them. They were completely ignored. The cowherds stood there for some time, they even reminded the *rishi*s that Krishna and Balarama had sent them, but it fell on deaf ears.

"Who is this Krishna and who is Balarama who orders us to feed these boys?" they thought. They did not know that the God for whom they were performing the ritual *yajna* was for Krishna, and Balarama was his elder brother.

The cowherd boys felt humiliated by the behaviour of the *rishi*s and became angry. They went back to Krishna and told him how they were humiliated by the *rishi*s when they asked for food, even after telling them that they were sent by Krishna.

Hearing them, the boys expected Krishna and Balarama to get angry but Krishna did not show any anger. He was calm and with a smile on his face, told them "friends! Let those *rishi*s be, don't think about them and do not get angry or disheartened by their behaviour. Go again there, and meet the wives of these inhospitable *rishis* and tell them the same thing and see what happens. When you mention my name you will see the response from those *rishi patnis* (wives of *rishis*)". So saying, he sent them on their way.

They reached the houses where the *rishi patnis* lived. Fortunately they were all together preparing to go to the forest where their husbands were. The cowherds stood in front of them and said "we are very hungry; Krishna and Balarama are also hungry and are waiting in Vrindavan for food."

The *rishi patnis* as soon as they heard the name Krishna and that he was hungry, at once got together tasty dishes and sweets. Dressing themselves up in their best clothes they were ready to go with the cowherds to where Krishna was. Some of them carried sandalwood paste and flower garlands for Krishna and Balarama.

The *rishi patnis* were walking in a procession carrying pots containing the food and other items, like fruits flowers, etc. . . . they came to the place where

their husbands, the *rishi*s, were performing the *yajna*. When the *rishi*s saw this strange spectacle of their wives following the cowherd boys carrying a lot of things, they could not believe their eyes.

They came running and stopped them and said "what is this you are doing? Where are you going carrying all this food, fruits and flowers? For whom? How dare you go without our permission and without informing us? Go back home at once," they commanded.

To this their wives replied, "we are not going back. Balarama and Krishna are hungry and we are taking food for them and for the cowherd boys. Kanha is a divine boy, he is god incarnated on this earth, and all those who belong to him are also divine. It is our privilege to serve him" and they walked on. Their husbands watched them helplessly.

Krishna was sitting under an *ashoka* tree with Balarama and some Gokul boys when the *rishi patni*s and the boys he had sent came to where he was. They saw the divine face of Krishna with an enchanting smile and beautiful black eyes twinkling with merriment, and saw divinity in him.

Krishna spoke to them, "I invoke the blessings of God on you for your kindness in coming here with food for us. Your husbands did not think it their duty to feed these hungry boys, but thought that by performing *yajna*s they could reach God. You are much more worthy of attaining the grace of God than your husbands. I bless you with all happiness and prosperity. I appreciate your generosity in feeding us. You have come here defying your husbands' commands. Go back and be of help to them in fulfilling their *yajna*, and may good fortune come to you" said Krishna and blessed them.

The women were overcome with devotion for Krishna and were reluctant to leave his divine presence. They felt they could live here for ever serving him and worshipping him. They were tongue-tied with emotion, only one among them boldly expressed their feelings. "O Krishna! we have given our hearts to you, how can you ask us to go back?" she said. Krishna's reply was to all of them, "you say you have given your hearts to me, when you say that does it not mean I belong to you?" Thus Krishna demonstrated what was true devotion and love which the *rishi patni*s had for him and his people, not the *rishi*s who performed *yajna*s without any love or devotion for God, nor for those poor, hungry friends of Krishna.

The *rishi*s also learnt a lesson that by mere ritualistic worship one cannot realize God.

7

The Wrath of Indra

The elders of Gokul were busy in preparations for the worship of Indra, the God of rain. Prosperity for farmers and cowherds means good rain, and for that they propitiated Indra every year in an elaborate *puja*.

This year too the preparations were under way and Krishna was present at a meeting of the elders. They included Krishna in their discussions, but Krishna sounded amused. Those gathered there did not understand his making light of the solemn occasion. Krishna then explained his views on the subject. His father Nandagopa was foremost among those who asked Krishna for his opinion on the scale of festivities to be organized that year. Krishna asked his father, "father please explain to me more about this annual *puja.* For whom are you doing it and for what purpose?" His father replied, "my son, it is good you asked me this question, as you should know about this *puja* which we perform every year. Lord Indra is the God of rain and the clouds and thunder; you know that for farmers and cowherds like us good rain in the proper season is essential for our prosperity. It is because of the grace of Indra that we are blessed with rain. We show our gratitude to Indra by worshipping him with all the farm produce. If we do not express our gratitude to Indra, misfortune may befall us." Thus Nandagopa explained to his son the purpose of this annual festival.

But Krishna did not accept this explanation. He decided to elucidate to his father and other elders who the true benefactors were who provided the farmers with rain, which would be beneficial. He said:

Dear father and respected elders,

you all know what *dharma* is, and about fate and the consequences of that which causes good and bad. Indra is not responsible either for rainfall nor for drought.

It is the people who by their virtuous deeds or by their evil deeds through their thoughts and actions determine their fate, that is to be prosperous and happy or to be poor and miserable. Indra is only a figurehead god, he can provide rain only if the people deserve it. The true providers of rain are the mountain ranges, the forests, and the living beings of this world. The fertile earth needs water, so there is rain.

If you want to show your gratitude for the rainfall and the plenty that comes with it show it to the true benefactors — the mountains, the forests, nature, all living beings and the good of mankind which make the skies bless you with rain.

This is what you should keep in mind. All the material you have collected for the worship of Indra, use it for worshipping nature. If there were no mountains with all its rich vegetation, no forests, no earth, and no living beings there would be no world. Understand this and give up your practice of propitiating Indra, and instead worship nature.

Thus Krishna convinced them of the futility of worship of Indra and enlightened them on the real benefactors, nature, and exhorted them to celebrate nature by worshipping the mountains.

Nandagopa was astounded at his son's convincing explanations. He agreed to worship nature in the mountains and give up propitiating Indra.

All the people of Gokul now gathered at the foot of the Govardhana Giri (mountain) and were preparing to celebrate nature and do *puja* to the mountains.

Why did Krishna stop the *puja* to Indra? There was a reason for this. Indra had become very arrogant and proud of his powers as the Lord of the three worlds. Krishna wanted to bring down his pride and teach him humility. No one can attribute greatness to himself.

The place surrounding Govardhana Giri was so beautiful, the water falls cascading from the mountains, the trees, the flowers, the greenery contributed to the scenery which was enchanting. Musicians were playing musical instruments; even the drums were soft and melodious. Heaps of food items for offering and later for the people to have as *prasad* were piled up. The aroma of delicious food and the sweet preparations filled the air. The festivities went on for five days, at the end of it one could see heaps and heaps of flowers, sweet smelling incense and food offering lying around the place. Nandagopa, Krishna, Balarama and all the people of Gokul returned home.

But in Indraloka, Indra was seething with anger and mortification that he was ignored by the people of Gokul, who did not perform the annual *puja* for him, instead they had worshipped the mountains and nature. He knew who was responsible for this, and to avenge the insult he called the clouds, and told them that "under the instigation of Krishna, the people of Gokul have insulted me, Indra, by denying me the *puja* which they have been hitherto conducting annually and have instead worshipped the mountains and nature. I command you to make incessant and heavy rain in Gokul and Vrindavan which would cause floods and the whole place and the people will drown in water." Indra's command was immediately carried out.

Suddenly in Gokul and Vrindavan the sky became dark, the sound of thunder was deafening and there was lightning, and the rain started pouring. It rained and rained for days without respite.

Life was at a standstill. The cries and wailings of the people struggling to keep alive could not be heard because of the sound of rain falling. People forgot their belongings which were floating in the water and were praying aloud to God to save them.

The only person who was calm was Krishna who stood smiling as if to say "when I am here why fear? Nothing can happen to you and nobody can destroy you." All the people came and surrounded Krishna. The divine smile of Krishna took away their fears and brought them hope. "Kanha," they said, "we have lost everything in the floods, we now only want to save ourselves, and only you can save us," and crowded round him.

Krishna did not reply to them but gestured to them to follow him. Krishna took them all to the Govardhana Giri on the outskirts of Vrindavan. There a miracle took place, Krishna became so strong he lifted the mountain Govardhana with one hand — some say by his little finger — and held it over the people. Not a drop of water fell on the people, cattle or anywhere.

Indra after seven days of incessant rain found that Krishna was holding Govardhana Giri aloft like an umbrella over the people of Gokul. He accepted defeat. The rains stopped, the clouds receded and the sun shone again over Vrindavan and Gokul.

Krishna put down the mountain and the people went back to their homes, singing the praises of their Kanha, who they realized was no ordinary boy, but Lord Narayana himself. Nandagopa, Yashoda and Balarama were full of love and pride for Krishna and went back to Vrindavan. Indra's pride was humbled and he came to Krishna and begged forgiveness.

Gopika Geetam

Once Krishna was playing his flute sitting under a tree on the banks of the Yamuna in Vrindavan. It was an enchanting scene, the trees and plants were swaying in the gentle breeze as if dancing to the music of Krishna's flute. The scent of sweet-smelling flowers wafted their fragrance in the breeze. A pale moon was peeping through the skies. All those who gathered there were silent, drinking in the beauty of the place and intoxicating music. Krishna's friends, the cowherd boys and some young *gopi*s of Gokul, had all come. The *gopi*s sat entranced as if a spell was cast over them.

Krishna in his usual pose was leaning against a tree his legs crossed and eyes closed was playing the flute the sweet melody of which had cast a spell on the *gopi*s.

The *gopi*s were so overcome with love at the sight of Kanha playing the flute, his curly hair flying in the breeze and his red lips pressed on the flute, that they could not control themselves. They came and surrounded him. The *gopi*s forgot their modesty; they forgot they were married and were supposed to stay away from the company of boys.

Krishna, who with his eyes closed, was absorbed in his playing, suddenly opened his eyes and saw a bevy of lovely damsels surrounding him, gazing at him with love-filled eyes. Krishna stopped his playing and said "O you *gopis*, what is this? Why have you come in the night without any escort? Don't you know that in the forest here there are demons and wild animals? Women should not venture out alone like this. What will your parents say if they come to know

of this? For those who love me I will give them joy and a good life, but I will not even dream of any harm coming to them. Go back, don't feel sad, be good, be virtuous, that is my advice," and he persuaded them to go back. But the *gopis* argued with him, "O Krishna, do not be so cruel and hard-hearted. Why do you drive us away? The whole world worships you. Can't we also be blessed with your love? Who else but you can abide in our hearts! We have come here to surrender ourselves to you. We want to always listen to the music from your magic flute. You have saved so many people from all kinds of dangers, why won't you save us?" thus they lamented.

Krishna was perplexed, he did not know how to console them. He suddenly noticed a beautiful form among the *gopi*s. She was unlike the others; she was quiet and did not utter a word. Krishna looked at her, and she smiled at him, the next second both of them disappeared from there. That beautiful *gopi* was Radha. Krishna and Radha walked some distance in silence, their love for each other was flowing within them. After walking for a long time Radha said "Krishna, my legs are aching please carry me," and she stooped a little in anticipation of being carried, but nothing happened.

She looked up and there was no Krishna, he had disappeared. Radha with tears pouring down her cheeks looked for her beloved everywhere but there was no sign of him. She walked back to the place from where he had taken her and saw the other *gopi*s crying at not finding Kanha. They all went in search of Krishna, singing his praises.

Suddenly he came and everything was bright. He danced with his Radha and the others danced round them. Then Krishna danced with each one of them, one Krishna for one *gopi*, the *gopika*s were in an ecstasy.

Who was this Radha? Why was she chosen by Krishna as his beloved? Radha was his close childhood playmate. Some say that she was Lakshmi, the consort of Lord Narayana and goddess of wealth. Not being able to bear the separation from her Lord she came among the *gopi*s as Radha. The dance of Krishna with the *gopi*s is celebrated as *Raas Krida* or *Raas Lila*. The love of Radha for Krishna was so deep that it filled her being. She felt she was always with Krishna. Some say that Krishna was married to Radha and his parents conducted the marriage, but there are so many versions that it is not possible to know which one is correct. Even now devotees of Krishna celebrate the marriage of Radha with Krishna, as Radha Kalyanam.

The *'rasa-lila'* of Krishna with Radha and the *gopi*s was rendered as a poetic composition called *Gopika Geetam* in circa tenth century in the Sanskrit text *Srimad Bhagavatam.*

8

Brave Deeds

The people of Gokul went to a place called Ambikavana to see the festival of Uma-Maheshvara which was being celebrated there. Ambikavana or Ambika forest was a beautiful place with its trees and flowers. The festival was celebrated in a grand manner. Krishna, Balarama and the Gokul boys were very happy and enjoyed themselves. Nandagopa invited the brahmans of Ambikavana and gave them a grand feast seeking their blessings for his sons Krishna and Balarama. Along with Nandagopa two other wealthy persons had also come. They were Upanandar and Chandanakar. The three of them decided

to host the forest feast that night. The place where all the people were sleeping after the feast was surrounded by dense forest.

While they were all fast asleep a huge snake came near the place where Nandagopa was sleeping and began swallowing the legs of Nandagopa and very soon would have swallowed all of him, when he awoke and screamed. The people came rushing with burning oil cloth torches and tried to kill the snake with sticks, and knives. But it went on swallowing Nandagopa, Krishna hearing the noise came running and seeing his father attacked by a snake kicked the snake with the strength of his feet and lo! A miracle took place. There was no snake, instead a handsome Vidyadhara (celestial being) stood there. Krishna asked him "O Vidyadhara, who are you? Who cursed you to be a snake?" The Vidyadhara replied with folded hands,

> Krishna, you have released me from a dreadful curse, I have no words to express my gratitude to you. My name is Sudarshan. One day I saw the great sage Angirasa Muni and on seeing him I laughed and mocked at his ugly face right in front of him. He became very angry and cursed me to be born a snake; when I pleaded forgiveness, he relented and told me, 'you will be released from your curse by Krishna who will be born in Gokul.' I have waited long for this day to regain my original form.

Krishna blessed him and the celestial being Sudarshan went away.

Nandagopa who was nearly swallowed by the snake recovered from the shock and they all happily returned to Vrindavan from Ambikavana.

The Death of Sangachuda

It was a full moon night. Krishna with Balarama and other *gopala*s and *gopika*s were in Vrindavan. Sometimes he would halt under a tree and play a flute, the others would sit down and listen enraptured by the divine melody that flowed from his flute. While they were enjoying themselves like this, Kubera's friend Sangachuda came that way. He was not a good person and when he saw the lovely *gopi*s listening with rapt attention and eyes closed, intoxicated by the divine music of Krishna's flute, he became jealous and wanted to possess the beautiful maidens for himself. By using his powers, he forcefully took the maidens with him. The *gopis* did not know how to get out of his clutches and cried out for Krishna to save them.

Krishna called out Sangachuda's name and asked him to stop, but Sangachuda ran on taking the *gopis* with him. Balarama in anger uprooted a tree and ran after him. Krishna with his divine powers went ahead of Sangachuda and was before him wherever he went. Seeing this Sangachuda got frightened and stopped.

Then Krishna raised both his hands together and gave him a stunning blow. That one fatal blow was enough to bring down the wicked Sangachuda. Krishna took from him a very precious ruby and gave it to his brother Balarama.

The Death of Arishtasura

Vrindavan did not remain peaceful for long. This time an *asura* bull by the name of Arishtasura made an appearance, determined to accomplish, what all the *asuras* sent by Kansa could not do, and that was to kill Krishna. Arishtasura, the bull, was a huge powerful beast, its long and piercing horns and long tail was indeed a terrifying sight.

The people ran to Krishna for protection. Krishna, who had saved them from so many dangers, Krishna, who lifted Govardhana Giri and held it aloft like an umbrella over the people and cattle of Vrindavan and humbled Indra, came out and faced the fierce bull. A young boy was preparing to fight a demon bull single-handed.

Krishna shouting war cries went near the bull, he put both his hands round the thick neck of the bull and squeezed it with all his might. Arishtasura shook

himself and with all his strength charged and attacked Krishna who, not being able to prevent the onslaught, fell down.

But immediately Krishna got up, anger welling within him, and caught hold of both the horns, shook the bull and flung him far away. Arishtasura lay still for some time, not being able to get up; he again tried to get up but again sank down. After several efforts he gave up. Krishna now came near him and killed him.

This great deed of Krishna's was hailed with admiration and gratitude by the people of Vrindavan. Thus Krishna and his brother Balarama performed many great deeds.

9

Coming of Akrura to Vrindavan

The great deeds performed by Krishna and his brother Balarama were conveyed to Kansa by the sage Narada, who was ever busy going round and giving information of what was happening in the world. Since he knew that King Kansa was mortally afraid of being killed by the eighth son of his sister Devaki, sage Narada paid a visit to King Kansa. Kansa had sent many *asura*s to kill the wonder-boy Krishna who was growing up as Nandagopa's son in Gokul, but Krishna had killed all the *asura*s sent by him.

Narada's purpose was to apprise Kansa of all the great deeds of Krishna and Balarama. Whenever Naradamuni chose to visit someone and convey information, it was not without a purpose. Thus the effect of his visit was to make Kansa rise up in fury and shout "I shall go to Gokul and cut off the heads of those two boys." Narada dissuaded him from doing any such deed.

"Kansa! Doing that is not such any easy task, their divine power and strength would help them to fight anyone who attacks them. You cannot do any harm to them. The only way you can save yourself is to mend your ways and give up your intentions of killing Krishna," said Narada and took leave of Kansa.

Kansa was disheartened but his anger was not less. In his anger he gave all kinds of orders. "Put Devaki and Vasudeva in prison," he ordered. He called for a cruel demon named Keshi and sent him to Vrindavan to kill both Krishna and Balarama.

He held a *durbar* and invited all his ministers, courtiers and advisors to be present, and consulted them about the ways and means to annihilate the two boys of Gokul.

He then took a decision; he dismissed the court and asked only his minister Akrura to stay back. He made him sit next to him. Now, Akrura was a very good, gentle and pious man, and Kansa wanted to make use of the goodness of Akrura to entice Krishna and Balarama to come to Mathura.

Kansa told Akrura,

> Akrura, I have tried with all my might and cunning to kill Krishna and Balarama, but have failed. I now want you to help me in bringing both of them here. By your wisdom and your ability you must persuade both of them to come with you to Mathura, after that I will deal with them. You must go to Vrindavan and tell Krishna that Kansa is conducting *dhanur-puja* and invite all his friends and relatives to attend the ceremony. You must personally invite Nandagopa and his family.
>
> You must bring Krishna and Balarama with you in your carriage, let Nandagopa and the others follow. This is all the help I ask of you, the troubles I have suffered because of Krishna cannot be counted. He killed Narakasura, Banasura, and Sambasura who were my close relatives and so many others. My hands are itching to kill him and revenge the deaths of all my people. So go to Vrindavan as my emissary and bring Kanha.

Kansa ended his lengthy command to Akrura. Akrura sat quietly listening to Kansa, he felt so sad that he had to do Kansa's bidding, but before he left he told him,

> O King Kansa! I cannot disobey you, having eaten your salt, and as your minister I am going on this mission. But let me tell you this, things will not happen the way you want. Good will triumph and evil destroyed. Remember you are fighting a divine power; no other power can stand against that divine power. I am warning you.

Thus giving Kansa a parting warning, Akrura left for Gokul.

Killing of Keshi and Vyoma

Meanwhile in Gokul Keshi, the demon, sent by Kansa to kill Krishna went there taking another demon named Vyoma. They had made a plan that at first only

Keshi would go and fight Krishna, in case he did not succeed in killing him Vyoma should come out and attack Krishna.

Keshi took on the form of a horse and came charging at Krishna, as he came he bit, kicked and tormented all those who were in his path, and when he came to Krishna he opened his mouth wide to swallow him, but Krishna put his hand in the horse's mouth and the hand grew so big that it tore the stomach of the *asura* Keshi and he fell down dead. Vyoma who was hiding and watching this came out to kill Kanha, but not as a demon. He very cleverly took the form of a boy and joined Krishna and the cowherds who were with him.

The boys were celebrating the killing of the demon Keshi and were playing and making merry, their cattle were grazing nearby.

Vyoma now started his work by dragging each one of the cowherd boys to a nearby rock cave. Now only five of them were left including Krishna and Vyoma. They realized that most of the boys were missing, and were worried, but only

Kanha was smiling. He quietly moved to where Vyoma, changed into a cowherd boy was standing. Krishna caught hold of his neck. A startled Vyoma became his true form of a demon and attacked Krishna, but Krishna's grip on his neck was very firm and with all his strength Krishna squeezed the life out of him. Vyoma went the way of Keshi.

Kanha and the remaining boys rushed to the cave and removing the rock released the other boys who were very happy to come out alive. This was another of the great deeds of Krishna.

Akrura's Journey to Vrindavan

Akrura was on his way to Gokul to carry out the orders of Kansa to bring Krishna and Balarama to Mathura. Throughout the journey his mind was fixed on Krishna. His heart was filled with joy at the thought that he was going to see the divine form of Krishna. He felt pity for Kansa who was under the impression that Krishna was an ordinary boy whom he could crush and kill. He did not know that his adversary was Lord of the universe and had the power to destroy anything and anyone at his will. He was sorry for Kansa who, by inviting Krishna to Mathura, was signing his own death warrant.

With all these thoughts running through his mind Akrura reached the banks of the Yamuna River in Vrindavan. Driving through the scenic beauty of Vrindavan with the Govardhana Giri as a backdrop to the river and the forests and lush vegetation and myriads of flowers, Akrura was enchanted by its beauty. It was dusk and the cattle were being driven home. The sound of women singing came floating in the air. Akrura raised both his folded hands and paid homage to Vrindavan and Gokul where Krishna had lived as a child, and then came to Vrindavan.

The chariot stopped in front of the biggest house in Vrindavan, almost like a palace. When they saw a grand carriage Nandagopa, Krishna and Balarama and the others surrounded the carriage. Akrura alighted from the carriage and accepted their greetings with folded hands.

Akrura saw Krishna and with great devotion touched his feet with his hands and put his hands to his eyes. He then greeted everyone there.

Nandagopa made all arrangements to welcome Akrura and a grand feast was prepared in his honour. After the feast Akrura was alone with Nandagopa, Krishna and Balarama in Nandagopa's house. Nandagopa enquired about the welfare of King Kansa. "O Akrura, is King Kansa well and prospering after killing all the children of Devaki and Vasudeva? The sins of his actions have caused great tragedies in Mathura and the people of Mathura are suffering. He has done great harm to us harassing us by sending *asura*s one after the other here, but let him be happy.

"We will talk about all matters tomorrow, you must now rest after your long journey," so saying Nandagopa and others left.

Coming of Akrura to Vrindavan

Only Krishna stayed back and sitting near Akrura's bed he asked him, "Akrura, are all my relatives well? Are my parents still in prison? And is Kansa causing them suffering? Do my parents know that you are coming to Vrindavan? and have they sent a message for me? Please let me know everything in detail. I want to know for what purpose Kansa has sent you here. Please tell me." Krishna thus plied Akrura with questions.

The nearness and presence of Krishna filled Akrura's heart with devotion.

Akrura apprised Krishna with all that was happening in Mathura, and the plan of Kansa in sending him to Vrindavan.

He addressed Krishna,

Krishna! You are born in the world to do good for mankind, but alas there is one who is born to do evil to you. That is his misfortune. One day Narada Muni came to see Kansa, he explained in detail the significance of your birth which was linked to Kansa's downfall and death. As soon as he heard this your uncle King Kansa wanted to kill your parents who had given birth to you. But some good sense prevailed and he ordered them to be imprisoned. But at the same time he took an oath that he would destroy you and your people, and would not stop till he had accomplished it.

He then with the advice of his evil counsellors planned to have a *dhanur-puja*. He sent me here to invite you, your brother and your father and all your relatives to Mathura to witness this great *yajna*. Once you all come to Mathura he will find ways and means to insult and torment you all.

He has called for the best and most vicious of wrestlers to fight you and Balarama.

As Akrura was saying all this, Krishna kept on smiling. Akrura went on, "Krishna, I know you are powerful enough to face even bigger troubles, but having eaten the salt of this wicked king I had to come on this mission." Krishna replied, "Very well, we shall leave tomorrow early morning for Mathura. Now dear Akrura, have your much needed sleep."

Next day, as soon as it was dawn Krishna and Balarama went to Nandagopa and told him that King Kansa had arranged a *dhanur-yajna* and had sent Akrura to invite them and others from Vrindavan to Mathura. "Brother and I will go ahead with Akrura and you all can follow."

Nandagopa at once called all his kinsmen and told them to be ready to leave for Mathura. "We should also take with us the annual tribute in gold and in kind to be paid to King Kansa." Even though the thought of seeing the wicked Kansa did not make them happy, the journey to Mathura was exciting, and they enthusiastically made preparations for the journey.

Krishna took leave of everyone, for in his heart he knew he would not come back to Vrindavan. The parting with all his friends and the good people of Vrindavan was deeply emotional. But for Krishna leaving his beloved Radha for ever was a poignant moment. Krishna gave her his flute which would always remind her of him. Krishna never played the flute after that. When Akrura took away Krishna from Vrindavan, Radha suffered intensely. but her love for Krishna was so sublime that she did not feel Krishna was going away from her because Krishna was in her. Thus she lived on in Vrindavan, never again to see her beloved Krishna.

The love of Radha and Krishna is celebrated by devotees of Krishna as Radha-Kalyanam, the marriage of Radha and Krishna.

10

Krishna Goes to Mathura

Akrura was on his way to Mathura with Krishna and Balarama. The whole of Vrindavan lined up on both sides of the street and watched Krishna and Balarama going till the carriage could be seen no more. The fear and empty feeling in the pits of their stomachs that Krishna might never come back made everyone's eyes wet.

Akrura stopped his chariot near the river Yamuna. Krishna and Balarama performed their ablutions and both of them waited near the chariot while Akrura went to the river to perform his.

While Akrura was praying standing in the water he had a divine vision of Krishna as Lord Narayana.

Akrura was overcome by emotion, his body was trembling, a pious and good man that he was, tears of joy were pouring down his cheeks. He could not believe his good fortune to have been blessed by the dazzling vision of the Lord. In ecstasy he raised both his hands high upon his head and standing in the water his mind concentrated on Krishna he lost count of time. It was only after a very long time that he came to himself, and regained consciousness. He opened his eyes and did not see the Lord there.

He walked to the carriage, and was greeted by Krishna, "Hey Akrura! What happened? You seem to have seen something which has made you look dazed?" and Krishna laughed mischievously. Akrura did not reply; he knew this was Krishna's doing, he merely smiled and drove the carriage.

On their way to Mathura they passed through many villages, and people thronged the streets to have a glimpse of Krishna and Balarama. Nandagopa and his relatives from Vrindavan, although they left later, reached earlier and halted in a beautiful spot and were camping there waiting for Akrura's chariot.

When Akrura reached that place Krishna asked him to stop the carriage. Krishna and Balarama got down, and Krishna told Akrura to go ahead to Mathura, and that they would join his father's party and reach Mathura. Akrura was unwilling to go without them and said, "Krishna, how can I leave you and go alone." Krishna replied "we will all come walking to Mathura and reach the palace. You go to your house, I promise you that before I leave Mathura, I will visit you and be your guest for a day," and so Akrura went on his way somewhat appeased.

Krishna and Balarama stayed with Nandagopa, Yashoda and the rest of the Vrindavan party. The next evening they left for Mathura. Mathura was not very far from there and very soon they could see the imposing buildings of Mathura.

The news had already reached the people of Mathura that Krishna was coming with a large party of people from Vrindavan and everyone was eager to see them. They were greeted with flowers and the *purna kumbham*, the traditional welcome with a brass pitcher of water in which were kept mango leaves and a coconut was placed in the centre.

As they were being given a grand welcome, Krishna noticed a *dhobi* standing in a corner. Krishna could see that he was puffed with arrogance. He was the *dhobi* for the royal family in the palace. Krishna decided to put him in his place. He called him and said "good fellow, you wash the clothes of King

Kansa and his family, isn't it? You must be an excellent *dhobi* to be employed as the palace *dhobi*. I want you to wash my clothes and the clothes of my people who have come with me as long as we are here, will you?," asked Krishna.

Having heard this, the *dhobi* became very angry, "who do you think you are to put yourself on a par with the royal family? You who are cowherds want me to wash your clothes? If King Kansa comes to know about this he will simply cut off

your heads," he said in a heated voice. His relatives, all *dhobis*, were standing near him with bundles of washed clothes.

Krishna lost his temper at the insolence of the *dhobi* and raised his hand and gave him a blow so hard that the man crumpled down on the ground. The other *dhobis* afraid that the same treatment would be meted out to them threw their bundles down and fled away. There was one among them named Sudama who did not run away but was gazing at Krishna with his hands folded with great devotion. Krishna went with Sudama to his house and enjoyed his hospitality. He then went to Kansa's palace. Sudama bade farewell to Krishna, garlanding him with flowers and showing his devotion to Krishna in many ways. Krishna thought more highly of Sudama's humble hut than of Kansa's palace.

11

Krishna in Mathura

The End of Kansa

Krishna, Balarama and the others from Gokul were walking towards the king's palace, when a young woman carrying a big cup of sandalwood paste was going in the same direction. She was beautiful, but had a stoop and was a hunchback. The strong scent of sandalwood filled the air. Krishna went and stood in front of the young woman and blocked her way, and asked her, "lady, for whom are you taking this strong scented sandal wood paste?" The young woman replied, "sir, I am a servant in King Kansa's palace. My name is Trivakra (she was also known as Kubja meaning hunchback). One of my duties is to grind sandal paste for the king and apply it on him. The king would not allow anyone else but me to bring him sandal paste."

Krishna then told her, "Trivakra, you are a very beautiful woman. Can you give some sandal paste for me?" The woman looked at him in amazement, and saw a captivating face with two enchanting eyes. "It is alright, you look like a person worthy of wearing this scented sandal paste on your body," and she gave the cup to Krishna. He applied the paste on his arms and chest and gave the cup to Balarama who also smeared it on his body.

Krishna returned the cup to Trivakra and told her, "you are young and beautiful but you have a deformity. I can remove the hunch from your back and make you straight, shall I?" The hunchbacked girl looked in disbelief at Krishna as if to say "can this be possible?" Krishna came near her and pressing her toes with his foot put his hands near her face and with a jerk straightened her. Now Trivakra the hunchback looked like a celestial maiden, she looked so lovely.

She bowed her head in gratitude before Krishna. The touch of Krishna had kindled in her heart a passionate love for him. "O Lord, how can I repay you for this great deed of yours, please come to my house and accept my love and devotion," she entreated. Krishna heard her and only laughed, "Thank you for your invitation, but I have no time, as we are all going somewhere else. I suggest you offer your hospitality to all the weary travellers who come this way. Blessing her, Krishna took leave.

All of them proceeded to the place where the *dhanur-puja* was being conducted. When they reached the place the guards standing there would not allow them to enter the pavilion. Krishna came forward and asked the guards, "will you or will you not allow us to enter?" This was asked laughingly and in a pleasant manner. The guards replied loudly, "no, we will not." Krishna sprang and picked up a huge bow and said "allow us to enter or you will lose your lives," and lifted the heavy bow and threw it on the ground and broke it. The breaking of the bow made a deafening noise which was heard in the *yajnashala* (the place where the *puja* was being conducted).

Kansa, who had anticipated all this by refusing Krishna and his people to enter, sent the giant wrestlers he had already stationed there to fight Krishna and Balarama. Now when the fierce wrestlers attacked them Krishna and Balarama each picked up a portion of the broken bow and rained blows on the wrestlers. Not being able to withstand the onslaught, the wrestlers fled away.

Krishna, Balarama, with Nandagopa and the others from Vrindavan turned back from the *yajnashala* and went to the outskirts of the Capital and camped in a garden. Now they knew the purpose of Kansa's invitation to them to come to Mathura.

They stayed on there first to find out what Kansa's plans were in regard to them. As for Kansa, from the day Krishna and his people entered Mathura Kansa was having bad dreams and nightmares, his mind was filled with the fear of forebodings of his death.

He prayed to God and his forefathers to save him. He arranged for special *puja*s and prayers in all the temples in his kingdom. He invited elderly, learned scholars, sages and godmen to his palace seeking their blessings for his long life.

Kansa heard that Nandagopa with Krishna and Balarama and the people of Vrindavan were camping on the outskirts of the city. He sent his emissaries to welcome them and bring them to his *durbar*.

Secretly he had arranged for wrestlers and ruffians to be hidden in the *durbar* hall.

In response to Kansa's invitation Nandagopa with his son Krishna and Balarama and the Vrindavan crowd all came to the huge hall where Kansa was holding *durbar.* As they were entering the hall a huge elephant named Kuvalayapida stood blocking their way. No one could pass through because of the elephant.

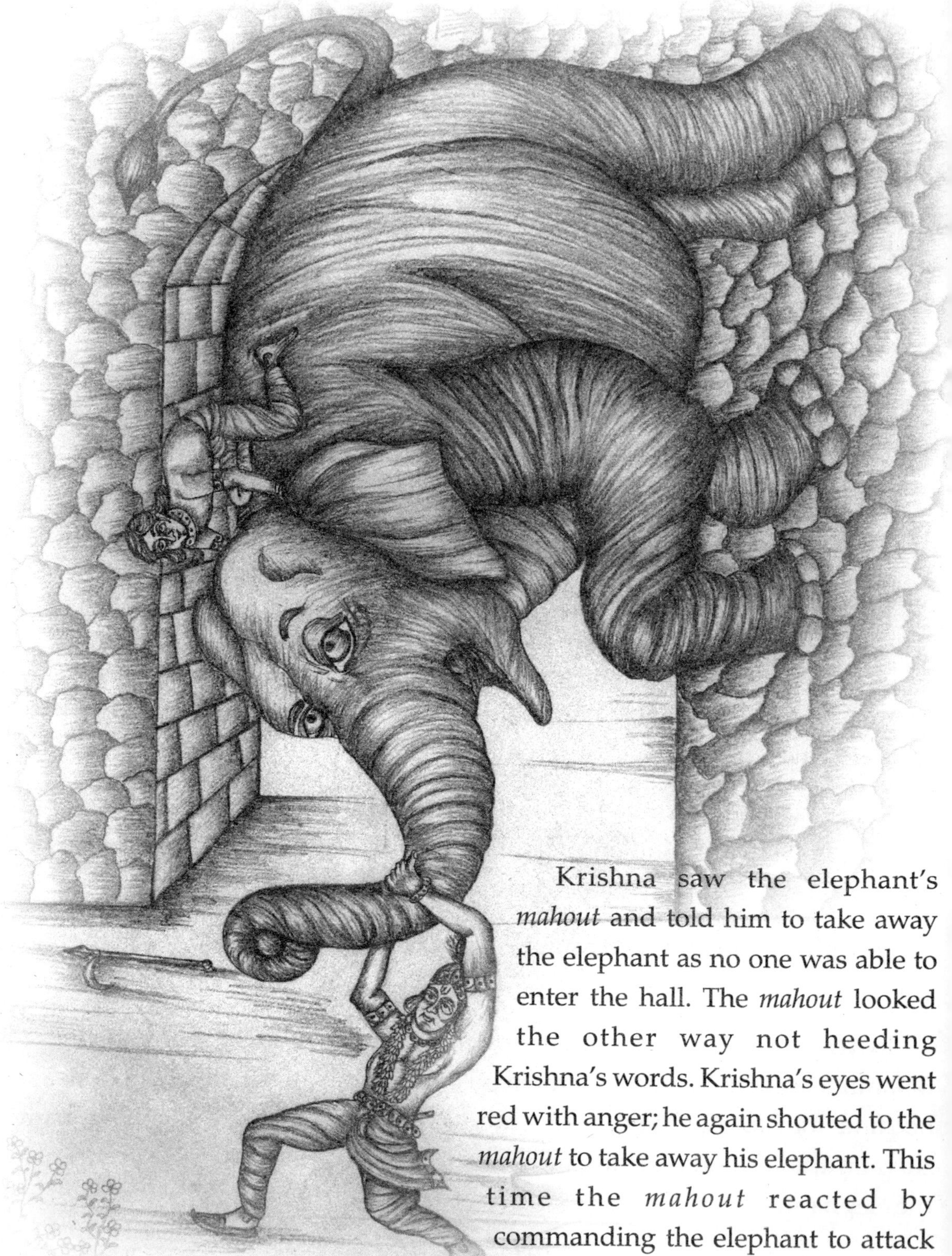

Krishna saw the elephant's *mahout* and told him to take away the elephant as no one was able to enter the hall. The *mahout* looked the other way not heeding Krishna's words. Krishna's eyes went red with anger; he again shouted to the *mahout* to take away his elephant. This time the *mahout* reacted by commanding the elephant to attack

Krishna. The huge Kuvalayapida elephant came charging with his tusk and swirling its trunk to lift Krishna but Krishna stepped aside and played a game of dodging the elephant. But the elephant trumpeting loudly came barging into Krishna. Then Krishna gave up his playing, and acted. His boyish arms acquired the strength of ten elephants and he caught hold of the ivory tusks of the huge elephant, twisted them, pulled them out and broke them into pieces. The elephant in pain ran as fast as his bulk could take him, the *mahout*s followed. In a little while the entrance was clear, no elephant, no *mahout*.

When Kansa heard that Krishna had broken the horns of Kuvalayapida the elephant, he lost hope of surviving at the hands of Krishna.

Krishna came to where Kansa was seated, carrying in his hands the broken tusks of the elephant.

Nandagopa and the others followed him. Those who were in the *durbar* were lost in contemplation of the divine face and form of Krishna but Kansa's reaction was different when he saw the brothers Krishna and Balarama. He saw his end in them. He immediately thought of another plan to kill them. Welcoming them he told them that he had heard of their prowess in wrestling, and had arranged a wrestling contest with some renowned wrestlers in his court. "It would be interesting to see who is stronger, the Vrindavan boys or the court wrestlers," he said.

Krishna and Balarama were silent. First two wrestlers, Chanura and Mustika, came forward and stood in front of them, crossing their arms and slapping their shoulders in readiness to fight.

Both the opponents fought fearlessly and were equally matched. Chanura took on Krishna and Mustika took on Balarama. Chanura and Krishna were

punching each other heavily and were rolling on the ground. The other pair, Mustika and Balarama, were bloodying each other with their punches.

Nandagopa and the others were watching the contest with anxious faces fearing for Krishna and Balarama. Kansa, on the other hand, was apprehensive of the fate of his two wrestlers. And just as Kansa feared, within a short while both Chanura and Mustika were lying on the floor, blood oozing out of their mouths. Krishna and Balarama stood victorious. Seeing the fate of Chanura and Mustika, the other wrestlers glided out of the hall noiselessly and escaped.

Now Kansa's fear for his life increased manifold. He became desperate, and ordered his army to capture or drive away all those who had come from Vrindavan. The soldiers at once went to where Nandagopa and the others were sitting and started beating them up.

Krishna, seeing his innocent people attacked by the soldiers, could not contain his anger and pulling out a sword he jumped on the dais where his wicked uncle was sitting. The next second he cut off the crown of Kansa which came rolling down. He then pulled him down from his throne, sat upon Kansa's body and squeezed the life out of him. Kansa died a slow painful death.

The great Kansa, who was ruling the kingdom with cruelty, injustice and tyranny, was at last silenced by the hand of God.

The people of Mathura were overjoyed to hear of the death of the tyrant King Kansa, and instead of mourning the death of their king they were celebrating.

Suddenly Kansa's *asura* brothers, eight of them, came to avenge the death of

Kansa, and attacked Krishna and Balarama. Balarama now forestalled Krishna and himself fought all the eight *asuras* with his weapon "Parikam," and sent them off to where their King Kansa went.

Thus Balarama single-handed killed the eight *asura* friends of Kansa.

Now Kansa's wives came weeping and stood before Krishna. Krishna consoled them and calmed them with soothing words.

Krishna then rushed to the prison where his parents were and freed them. Devaki and Vasudeva were in awe of their son's divinity, they knew he was not an ordinary boy but God incarnated on earth, and they raised folded hands to him and bowed to him.

Krishna did not want his parents to feel he was God and have respect for him, he wanted to be their child to be hugged and kissed by them. So by his *maya* he

removed from their minds the knowledge that he was divine, and made them feel love for him as their son.

Krishna's next act was to free his ageing maternal grandfather, Maharaja Ugrasena, and bring him to the palace and restore to him his kingdom. King Ugrasena now ruled over Mathura.

Krishna was now faced with the poignant moment of parting from his beloved parents Nandagopa and Yashoda who had brought him up with such love. He loaded them with costly presents like gold, pearls, gems and everything that he could possibly think of. He told them that Balarama and he would stay back in Mathura, but would always remember his parents and the people of Vrindavan and Gokul with love and gratitude. Nandagopa and Yashoda had to accept the inevitable and were grateful for those precious days their lovely Krishna spent with them. With their hearts filled with sorrow at the parting from their beloved son and from Balarama they left for Vrindavan.

Thus ends this story of Krishna born to Devaki and Vasudeva and brought up by Nandagopa and Yashoda in Gokul, where his babyhood and his childhood as a cowherd boy was spent, the darling of his parents, the darling of the *gopi*s and the beloved of Radha. Krishna never went back to Gokul, or Vrindavan.

The story of the divine child Krishna ends here. The role of Krishna as the king of Dwaraka and the charioteer of Arjuna in the great battle of Kurukshetra and most significantly, the preaching of the *Bhagavad Gita* relates to the life of Krishna as Dwarakadheesh. This is the core of the epic *Mahabharata* while *Srimad Bhagavatam* tells of Krishna Lila.

SUBHAM